His
Healing
Peace

Tony Cubello

Queen of Peace Healing Ministry
Buffalo, New York

His Healing Peace
by Tony Cubello

Queen of Peace Healing Ministry
Buffalo, New York

For additional copies, write:
P.O. Box 14
Niagara Falls, NY 14304

ISBN #0-9688426-8-2

Printed by:
Ave Maria Centre of Peace,
Toronto, Ont.

Dedication

To the Holy Trinity

God, The Father

God, The Son

God, The Holy Spirit

From whom comes all Love, Grace, Peace and Healing

and

To Mary, The Mother of God

with her words:

"Do whatever He tells you"

ACKNOWLEDGMENTS

I am grateful to:

Msgr. George Yiengst for reviewing the manuscript and for allowing my ministry to conduct monthly healing services at St. Pius X Church for these past ten years.

Charlene McGraw for her uncanny ability to decipher and transfer my handwriting into typewritten form and for all other assistance pertaining to the publishing of this book. Most of all Charlene, may God bless you with more gifts and graces, as He continues to use you in a powerful way to bring honor and glory to His Holy Name.

Dominique Sanchez for all her work in formulating the manuscript for publication.

All the pastors for inviting this ministry to perform healing services at their respective parishes.

All the diocesan and religious priests who have celebrated or con-celebrated our masses, not only at St. Pius X Church, but also at various churches where we have conducted healing services.

Marians of the Immaculate Conception for use of quotations from St. Faustina's Diary, Divine Mercy in My Soul © 1987 and the Image of St. Maria Faustina Kowalska, courtesy of the Congregation of Marians of the Immaculate Conception, Stockbridge, MA 01263. Used with permission.

Talented Artist, Terry Gellart for all the artwork contained in this book (with the exception of the above and image of St. Michael the Archangel - courtesy of Josyp Terelya).

DECLARATIONS

I, hereby, acknowledge that this is God's book as:

The scripture passages contained herein, are the inspired words of the Holy Spirit to His disciples.

"All Scripture is inspired by God and is useful for teaching the truth, rebuking error, correcting faults, and giving instruction for right living," (2 Timothy 3:16)

Private revelations contained in this book are from Our Lord and Our Lady and were received in the form of interior locutions.

"Do not restrain the Holy Spirit; do not despise inspired messages. Put all things to the test: keep what is good and avoid every kind of evil". (1 Thessalonians 5:19-21)

My own thoughts and reflections were inspired through prayer and meditation, mostly with the accompaniment of a lighted, blessed candle. As I wrote these thoughts, I also chose and added the messages given to me by Jesus and Mary that pertain to the subject matter, in most of the chapters in this book.

The messages received from Our Lady will be noted, all other messages are from Jesus.

The author recognizes and accepts that the final authority regarding these messages rests with the magisterium of the Roman Catholic Church.

Testimonies from witnesses of various reported healings are also included.

FORWARD

Oft times, I read over the pages of the New Testament and am amazed at the effect a few men had on our world. I wonder to how many they really preached the Good News, that Jesus Christ has come to save us. That we do not know. Yet their message still influences our world two thousand years later.

Throughout the history of the Church, there have been many who have had an effect on people. I think of St. Francis of Assisi, St. Therese, and St. Padre Pio, just to name a few.

In his small way, the compiler of this little spiritual gem, Tony Cubello has had an impact on many people. He is neither priest nor preacher. He is a layman, a vessel of clay filled with the Holy Spirit. Having read the testimonies in this book, his healing ministry must surely be blessed in heaven.

I enthusiastically welcome this opportunity to recommend this book and pray for Tony's continued success in his mission of assisting people to grow in the likeness of Christ and to seek out His Divine Mercy. "Jesus, I Trust in You".

Rev. Msgr. George B Yiengst,
Pastor of St. Pius X Church
Getzville, New York

INTRODUCTION

(How This Book Came To Be)

One evening after mass and while reciting the Rosary, in a little church where many prayers are said, I began to experience what seemed to be flashbacks of my past spiritual journey. I didn't understand this, because I usually would receive messages during the quiet time of adoration, following the recitation of the Rosary. Then, while adoring Jesus, I asked Him about what was meant by the thoughts given to me during the Rosary.

He said, in what seemed to be in a "ticker tape" thought:

(489) 4/1/93

YOU SHALL WRITE A BOOK! It will be as your thoughts, for it will contain true facts and revelations to increase the faith of My people. Keep in mind that it is for the edification of My people, but primarily it will be for My glory. I WILL HELP YOU!

I then recalled previous messages that I did not understand at the time that I received them.

(115) 1/1/92

Be obedient in all I ask of you to do. You will be recounting this story at a later date, for the edification of others.

(450) 2/13/93

All I say to you will be related one day.

A few days later, while in prayer and after pondering at length these events, I again meekly asked Jesus, "Lord why am I to write this book?" His answer was, **"BECAUSE IT WILL TOUCH HEARTS!"** I did not question further.

If any part of this writing opens your heart to Jesus, thank Him for this grace, as He and He alone is to be the recipient of all praise, honor and glory.

TABLE OF CONTENTS

NEW BEGINNINGS

It was in July of 1991 that Our Lord and Our Lady began speaking to me; however, most of the messages I received were from Jesus. They were not audible voices, but soft, still voices within my heart, which reflected thoughts to my mind. I did not understand, but somehow knew, that I was to write down what was being related to me.

The first site of this experience was at Our Lady of Fatima Shrine in Lewiston, New York. I was sitting on a bench facing the replica of the original chapel in Fatima, Portugal, where in 1917, Our Lady appeared to the children, Lucia, Jacinta and Francisco at the place known as the Cova da Iria. I received other messages at this location, as well as before the Blessed Sacrament, in churches, in my car, in my room and other sites.

The Lord was preparing me to be His instrument of healing and so He began teaching me. Along with these teachings for the ministry of healing, I was also receiving messages regarding others and for humanity. Since 1991 to date, I have received over 1440 pages of messages from Jesus and Mary.

The following are some of the messages pertaining to ministry:

(2) 7/20/91

I am calling you to a higher ministry, My son. This ministry will be based on love and understanding.

(5) 7/21/91

I will come to you, from time to time, and let you know of My Will for you.

(6) 7/21/91

Align yourself with My Holy Mother, she will lead you.

(7-8) 7/24/91

In the course of the next few days, meditate on the mysteries of the Rosary, they will tell you much. Learn of My attachments, My detachments. We will have a love connection, you and I. "Peace" is the key word, My son.

(9-10) 7/26/91

I will be all things to you, comforter, friend and listener. I have brought you into this work for a purpose - to win souls for Me. My Spirit will fall upon you and bring you graces untold.

(13-14) 7/28/91

Let My Spirit work in you and through you. You are a chosen disciple to do My work. You will be called to be united with My Blessed Mother. There will be work for you to do. I call the broken, the wounded healers, for My witnessing. You are the candidate I have chosen.

(15) 7/29/91

Transform your mind to the level of holiness. Look to the hills of Medjugorje, for there you will find My Holy Mother.

I had already made three pilgrimages to Medjugorje and was preparing for a fourth pilgrimage in September of 1991.

(17) 8/2/91

Our Lady

Be at peace my son, for you will be with me in Medjugorje. There my heart will speak to your heart.

I asked the Lord why He chose to speak to me. His reply:

(19,21) 8/4/91

You come seeking, that is why I reveal Myself to you. I want you to be a soldier for Me, a catalyst in the ministry that I have prepared for you. Be open to My Holy Spirit. Let all that I have said to you begin your new life — life in My Spirit.

(25-27) 8/7/91

You come to Me for direction, My son, but I have been directing you all along. I will teach you, one day at a time. It is not My Will to teach you too much, too soon. I will give you a gift, a heavenly gift. Use it with wisdom and knowledge.

(28,30) 8/10/91

I am entrusting to you, a key that will open the hearts of My people ready for Me to enter. It is not beyond Me to do this if I so choose. We, you and I, must carry on the work of the Father. I calmed the seas, I calm your spirit. You calm My people.

(35) 8/14/91

I will speak to you in many different ways.

(37,39) 8/19/91

You have already been given the gift, it lies within you. You are coming to Me as a child and that is as it should be. No other way will do.

(40-41) 8/21/91

My heart seems to want more of you, My son. I am

calling you to give more of yourself. The road to holiness is giving. Be of glad heart when you are lonely, for it is then that I can work best in you.

Seek out the lonely, the helpless, those in need.

(42) 8/23/91

All of this is the task I ask of you, for My Honor and Glory. Do not count the cost, I will tally the figures. When all is done, all will be well.

(46-47) 8/24/91

I illuminate the sky with stars. I illuminate your soul with Me. Be courageous, lest you falter. My rod and My staff will support you. Conduct yourself in a manner befitting a Christian. Let all who see you know that you are mine.

(54-55) 9/1/91

I will give to you the key to ministry, it will come naturally. I need you and I will lead and give you whatever is necessary to complete this learning process. I will send you deeper into Wisdom and Knowledge. Love is akin to compassion, that is what is needed for the ministry I have prepared for you.

(58-64) 9/6/91

Lay your hands gently upon them. It will seem as though I ask much of you, but I will give you much in return. As I lead you to My people, I will prepare you.

Be concerned not of what to do or say, for it will be Me working through you. My Spirit will do the leading, you will be but a follower.

Be an instrument — no, a broken vessel in My

Hands and let Me repair you, mold you and make you exactly what I want you to be and then only, will you become an instrument of My Power.

I cannot use the proud and the mighty, but I can use the humble and the lowly. I have chosen to direct and correct you and make you purified in the fire.

You cannot carry My Cross; however, you can help carry a splinter of it.

I am eternal, I am everlasting. I Am Who Am! Listen to My Words. Heed My Words, for it is such as you, who will carry on My works.

My little one, I have chosen this avenue for you, because you are pliable in My Hands. I have established this rapport with you to complete the purpose for which you are to be used.

I do not choose unwisely, so be alert to new beginnings. I will share the thoughts, you will do the works. My Spirit will direct, you will animate. I have told you that I need those who would persevere in My Name. Close all former doors and let Me open new doors. I see you as one who I will use to do these works, in spite of your weaknesses, for I prefer the weak and not the strong. The weak bend, but the strong hold fast to the world. Look to Me and for Me, as I am but a breath away.

(66-67) 9/8/91

Listen to My soft, still voice. I will lead you on a path which would seem unusual to you. Go deepen your faith, deepen your commitment to Me and let the harmony flow between us.

It took a long time before I could understand why Jesus and Our Lady spoke to me in this manner, but I have since learned that they speak to many people, especially to those who will pray and listen for the small, still voice within their hearts.

As to some explanation of the writing of these messages: most of the time before I could finish a sentence, I was given the next sentence, so that there was no time to "cross the T's" or "dot the I's", which I did at the end of the messages. I was given some words that I had never written or used, but somehow was able to spell correctly. The language given to me was sometimes words of old, as well as today's jargon. In all of this was the awesome ways that Our Lord would confirm these messages; through Holy Scripture, Christian literature, homilies, church bulletins, people, circumstances, etc..

Our God is an amazing God and I thank Him for saving us, for being with us and for sending His Holy Mother to guide and protect us.

THE MESSAGE OF MEDJUGORJE

On each of my pilgrimages to Medjugorje, I encountered different experiences. On my first trip, for some reason, I was not able to join the group to climb Apparition Hill (Podbrdo). This site is where the Blessed Virgin Mary is reported to have first appeared to the six children from this little Croatian village on a daily basis since 1981. Most know them by their first names: Mirjana, Ivanka, Vicka, Maria, Ivan, and Jakov.

The next day, while two of my companions stayed behind looking to purchase rosaries and medals in the small shops below the hill, I commenced to ascend Apparition Hill. In spite of the rocky terrain, I had the sensation that my feet were not touching the ground. When I reached the top, I prayed, meditated and took in the beautiful view of St. James Church and Mount Krizevac, the other two focal sites of Medjugorje. On the way down however, I did feel the stony path beneath my feet. When I met up with my companions, they asked why I had remained on the hill for so long. I thought I was there for a half-hour or so; in reality, I was gone for 2-1/2 hours.

I felt very serene, within myself and, in a way, perhaps as Moses felt when he descended from the mountain; however, I am not comparing myself with Moses. The peace I experienced on Apparition Hill was so overwhelming that I wanted to remain there and drink in the love of Jesus and Mary.

On this same visit to this "haven of peace", we were outside St. James Church facing Cross mountain (Mount Krizevac), because the church was filled to capacity. At the time that Our Lady was appearing to the children, I saw a reddish pink cloud covering the 35-foot cross on the mountain and as the cloud dissipated, I observed the cross slowly turning. Had I been alone, I probably would have thought that I was hallucinating, except that 80 or so others had also viewed this same sight. On my last pilgrimage to Medjugorje, I saw the Cross on Mount Krizevac, not turning as before, but actually spinning and then, as if this were not breathtaking enough, the cross began to disappear and reappear. A member of our pilgrimage recorded this phenomenon on video.

It is not the signs and wonders that make up Medjugorje, although I believe that, at times, God uses these phenomena to get our attention, but it is the messages given by Our Lady, through the visionaries, for all of humanity that is the true spirit of Medjugorje.

The messages emanating from Heaven which will bring us closer to the Sacred Heart of Jesus and to the Immaculate Heart of Mary are **FAITH, PRAYER, FASTING, PENANCE, CONVERSION AND PEACE.**

(55) 9/1/91

You will find something in Medjugorje that you have been seeking.

(58,61) 9/6/91

It is there (Medjugorje) that I will lay the foundation of this new ministry.

Listen to the words of My Holy Mother, when you are there. She will speak to your heart. You will hear her in the center of your peace.

(68-70) 9/18/91

I come to you now on the Hill of Apparitions, where My Holy Mother appears. You are to get to know Her and let the world know of her. She comes as My emissary to speak to the world of My love for them. They are to listen to her words for they are the words of My Father.

Be truth to them and let them know of My truth. My truth, My Way and My life. You will see and hear much of My life, here, in this Holy Place.

I will bring peace to you, here in Medjugorje. I will bring peace to those others who have come with

open hearts.

Let the peace I bring you be transferred to others, as you leave this Holy Place of Worship.

(95) 11/4/91

Our Lady

I was happy when you came to see me in Medjugorje. We are growing closer, you and I. I want to know you better also.

(129) 2/12/92

Keep faith with the people of Medjugorje.

Pray for them.

Pray for all of Yugoslavia.

Our Lady is God's messenger of these times and what better way to Jesus than through His Mother Mary.

CALLED INTO SERVICE

I have made several pilgrimages to Medjugorje, a small village in the middle of the former Yugoslavia (Republic of Bosnia-Herzegovina). It is in this remote mountain area in 1981 that the Blessed Virgin Mary began appearing to six children, now adults, on a daily basis. It has been now over twenty-two years.

It was on my fourth pilgrimage to Medjugorje in September of 1991 that a visiting priest, who was being used as an instrument of healing, had ministered on this particular afternoon to some 5,000 to 6,000 people, mostly native Croatians. That evening, he came to where the members of our pilgrimage group were staying. This building had a dining area that accommodated the 40 or so people that were gathered for a small healing service.

First, we prayed, then Father and a lay person, both operating in the gifts of the Holy Spirit, began to speak as the Lord led them. There was revelation of various illnesses and emotional problems. In particular, someone was not able to visit the final resting place of a loved one who had passed away three years prior and now was given the grace to overcome this problem. This healing was later proven to be true. Then came words from the priest that there were some in the room who would be used as instruments of healing. At these words, my spirit was moved and I experienced mixed feelings.

Some months later, after returning home from Medjugorje, I learned that this same priest was on retreat in Canada and that he was having a healing mass at a church some 60-70 miles from where I lived. Imagine my surprise, that this priest whom I met in Medjugorje and who travels the entire globe in his ministry was coming to a location within driving distance from where I resided. Three of us attended this healing mass: Rev. Bob Rezac, a friend and myself.

The next day, I received a call from the healing priest. He said that shortly I would be praying over people, as an instrument of healing and that this word was Divine Revelation of the mission for which I was chosen. Soon thereafter, I was asked to pray over a small group at a little church following the mass. The pastor at this parish had been to Medjugorje and has a profound devotion to Our Lady. Next, I was asked to pray over a prayer group of 120 or more at a convent chapel in Williamsville, New York.

One day, Charlene McGraw, a member of my ministry and a parishioner at St. Pius X Church in Getzville, New York, and I were led to approach the pastor, Rev. Msgr. George Yiengst. We asked him if we might conduct a healing service at St. Pius X Church. We told him that I would be laying hands on those attending, if they were open to this. Somehow, there was a mix-up and instead of agreeing to one healing mass, we were scheduled for three healing masses. I believe the Holy Spirit was working within this Pastor and that God had pre-pared him to receive us, just as He had prepared me for this ministry. These masses have continued, monthly, and we have now completed our tenth year conducting healing services at this church.

The fruits of these healing masses have been reflected in reported physical and emotional healings, and, of course, the most beautiful healings of all, the spiritual healings in which people have had conversions to Jesus, and for others, a deeper walk in their faith.

There will be more elaboration regarding these fruits, in a later chapter on testimonies.

MEDJUGORJE

A Message of Peace, Conversion, Faith, Prayer, Fasting and Penance

The story of Medjugorje begins on June 24, 1981, when six teenagers reported that they had encountered the Blessed Virgin Mary on a hillside near the village. The children described the lady as being very young and indescribably beautiful, possessing dark hair and blue eyes. Dressed in gray and white, she wore a white veil with a crown of stars appearing above her head. On the third day of the apparitions, the teenagers asked who she was, and the lady replied, "I am the Blessed Virgin Mary".

Signs and miracles have been very evident at Medjugorje. In those early days after June of 1981, when the Medjugorje parish was the scene of communist authorities, the word "MIR" (Croatian for "Peace") appeared in the sky, witnessed by thousands. On the top of Mt. Krizevac, the highest mountain in the area, which is located just behind St. James Church, the villagers erected a 35-foot cement cross commemorating Our Lord's death and resurrection. On numerous occasions, people have seen the cross pulsating with light or spinning, or surrounded by a great golden glow.

A common occurrence, witnessed by many thousands, is seeing the sun change colors, spin, and become a silver disc pulsating in the sky. There have been many reported physical healings, but the most important wonders have been the spiritual healings: conversions, people changing their lives and reconciling with God and with each other. Countless thousands have suddenly found their faith and their God in Medjugorje.

Healing
Mass
St. Pius X
Roman
Catholic
Church

Rev. Msgr. George B Yiengst, Pastor of St. Pius X Roman
Catholic Church, Getzville (Diocese of Buffalo), New York

Apparition Hill where the young visionaries first encountered Our Lady.

Krizevac (Cross) Mountain, where in 1933 the villagers built a 35 foot cross on the 1900th Anniversary of Jesus' Crucifixion.

St. James Church, Medjugorje

AND ALSO, THE CROSS

Jesus tells us, throughout Holy Scripture, that there will be persecution and suffering for those who follow Him:

> *"Whoever does not take up his cross and follow in my steps is not fit to be my disciple." (Matthew 10:38)*

> *"Then Jesus said to his disciples, "If anyone wants to come with me, he must forget himself, carry his cross, and follow me". (Matthew 16:24)*

> *"All I want is to know Christ and to experience the power of his resurrection, to share in his sufferings and become like him in his death..." (Philippians 3:10)*

> *"My dear friends, do not be surprised at the painful test you are suffering, as though something unusual were happening to you. Rather be glad that you are sharing Christ's sufferings, so that you may be full of joy when his glory is revealed." (1 Peter 4: 12,13)*

> *"Everyone who wants to live a godly life in union with Christ Jesus will be persecuted..."(2 Timothy 3:12)*

I, and those in my ministry, have come to know the meaning of the above passages of Holy Scripture. We have all experienced, in some way, spiritual, physical and emotional suffering and persecution. There is no easy way along the road to Calvary, but the consolation is that we may be enjoined to Him by perhaps carrying a splinter of His Cross.

Jesus and Mary's words to me in conjunction with the above:

(23) 8/5/91

I have called you to holiness but with it, goes the Cross. Lean your head on My shoulder as John did, and I will console you.

(74) 9/30/91

Let any suffering that you experience here on earth be offered up to Me, your Lord and your God.

(87) 10/26/91

Learn of suffering, learn of Me.

(99) 11/24/91

The deceiver is working feverishly to accomplish his evil deeds. I will not let you falter.

Bless yourself much with Holy Water and cover yourself with My Precious Blood.

(126) 2/12/92

Like Job, I can end your term, if you wish, or like Job, you can remain My servant.

(128) 2/12/92

I challenge you to persevere as I will not let you go through the valley of darkness alone. I will be with you, every step of the way.

(131) 2/21/92

Believe in the cause of suffering, for I want you for a victim soul. St. Therese and others have gone through this, I have used them for this purpose.

(138) 3/11/92

Gladly embrace this suffering, as you will be joined with Me.

(167) 5/10/92

Our Lady

My heart is sensitive to your heart. The heartaches are not in vain. Did I not have heartaches when they took my Son? When they crucified Him? When I held His limp body in my arms?

(299) 9/25/92

Be at peace, be at prayer, be love to one another. Be Me to your neighbor, accept suffering, accept the Cross. Then you can say, "I am a son of the Most High".

(342) 10/18/92

It hurts, does it not?

Imagine how I felt when My friends turned on Me. No one, but My Mother and a few others stayed with Me. No one cared. Not many care today. I keep calling to them and hoping that they will answer My call. You have had but a taste of My Passion.

(343) 10/19/92

Know that all My Saints have suffered in the same way. This is My path for those of whom I choose. Be thankful that you are among the chosen. I ask for your services and it is up to your free will, whether or not, you will serve Me.

(394) 12/1/92

These days of indecision are the most difficult, are they not? They are meant to be, for through all of this, My poor souls are being saved. This is your offering for them.

Be elated, for you are doing the works of the suffering. More will come your way; more souls will be saved. Your reward will be a hundred-fold in My Kingdom. Offer up all to Me that is displeasing to you. You will be imbued with My Spirit, as you encounter all challenges, in My name. The burden is upon Me, for the works of the Spirit, not upon you; therefore be at ease and let all take place in My time.

(588-590) 7/31/93

Our Lady

Listen, always, to the words of my Son, for His words are words of truth. What you are going through will be Honor and Glory to Jesus, for through your suffering, emerges the saving of countless souls for the "Lamb of God".

Persevere to pray in the churches that come to mind and step out in faith and ask in boldness.

Let not my adversary take hold of you, as he attempts to taunt and tempt my little ones. Invoke the Precious Blood of my Son, come under my Mantle of Protection and call upon the Court of Heaven and no harm will befall you or the others of which are united to you in Christian love and in service to my Son.

(755-756) 6/12/94

Our Lady

I allow you to become part of my cohort of these last times.

You are of those united to my Immaculate Heart and to the Sacred Heart of my Son. You will be called upon to suffer, sacrifice and pray so that others may live in eternal life. Be thankful that you have been called out of this world to be among the chosen. Your life now belongs to my plan which will bring

many souls to my Divine Son. Rejoice when you suffer, for it is then that you know that you belong to my Son and I. I long for a more intimate relationship with you as you have indicated that you want to know more of me. This will come to pass.

We are one in prayer as you minister to those who seek my Son with needs. More prayer, fasting and praise of my Son, is my request of you and of my children, bonded together with you, in union with the Trinity.

Let us all stand beneath the Cross, together. It is a privilege for each one of us to serve our great God in any ministry, and to follow Him in our daily lives, but know this, with it goes "the Cross".

GOD IS STILL HEALING

When Jesus ascended into Heaven, we became heirs to the legacy of His healing power.

"I am telling you the truth: whoever believes in me will do what I do – yes, he will do even greater things, because I am going to the Father." *(John 14:12)*

"I have told you this while I am still with you. The Helper, the Holy Spirit, whom the Father will send in my name, will teach you everything and make you remember all that I have told you." *(John 14:25,26)*

One avenue for the above is to be accomplished by the "laying on of hands", with prayer, calling upon the Name of the Lord, for the healing power of His Holy Spirit.

"When they arrived, they prayed for the believers that they might receive the Holy Spirit. For the Holy Spirit had not yet come down on any of them; they had only been baptized in the name of the Lord Jesus. Then Peter and John placed their hands on them, and they received the Holy Spirit."

(Acts 8: 15-17)

Jesus wants to heal us and be whole in body, mind and spirit. However, all healing is according to His Divine Will, as He knows what is best for us so that we may bathe in the waters of salvation.

"This is what I will do in the last days, God says:
I will pour out my Spirit on everyone.
Your sons and daughters will proclaim my message;
your young men will see visions,

and your old men will have dreams.
Yes, even on my servants, both men and women,
I will pour out my Spirit in those days,
and they will proclaim my messages." (Acts 2: 17,18)

".... Go throughout the whole world and preach the
gospel to all mankind....believers will be given the
power to perform miracles .... they will place their
hands on sick people and these will get well". (Mark
16: 15-18)

The previous passages are but a few taken from Holy
Scripture. The bible is laced with accounts of healing by Jesus
and His disciples. This inheritance of God's gift of healing represents His love and compassion for His people. By His stripes,
His grace, and His mercy we can be healed. We have but to follow His precepts and adhere to the two great commandments:

"Love the Lord, your God with all your heart, with all
your soul, with all your mind, and with all your strength.
The second most important commandment is this: Love
your neighbor as you love yourself. There is no other
commandment more important than these two".

(Mark 12: 30,31)

HEALING POWER OF GOD

The gift of healing is merely the power of God working through a person to bring another to health in body, mind and spirit. When we lay hands upon one another in prayer we are God's instruments of healing, love and compassion. Jesus uses us in this way, as He is now a Spirit and, therefore, utilizes our voices to pray and our hands to impose on one another. He does this to bring about healing and peace to His people.

During the "laying on of hands", people may be seen "Resting in the Spirit", that is those who are overcome by God's Holy Spirit and are falling back, as "catchers" (men standing behind persons being prayed over), gently ease them to the floor. This experience encompasses various manifestations of God's Holy Spirit. At this time, one is intimately touched by God's love accompanied by His healing power.

If while being prayed over a person does not experience the manifestation of Resting in the Spirit, it does not mean that God has not touched that person in a special way. It is possible to experience His healing touch the next day or at a later time. When approaching to receive prayers for healing one should come with an open heart, and preferably, following a good confession as RECONCILIATION WITH GOD IS THE BEGINNING OF ALL HEALING.

Some people come "under the power" of God without the person who is laying on hands being anywhere near them. Perhaps, this is one way that our Lord demonstrates to us that He is in control, that it is His power manifesting itself and, perhaps, His way to keep us humble.

The ministry of healing has been entrusted to priests in a special way by the Church through ordination. Only priests can administer the sacrament of Anointing of the Sick. However, some people have the gift of healing directly from God and should not be prevented from using it because this gift has been given to them for the good of all.

THE PRIESTHOOD

Many priests have influenced my spiritual journey, but one in particular has had a tremendous impact on my life. I met Father Matthew Swizdor, a Franciscan priest, early on in my ministry. He befriended me and we had several discussions on spirituality and healing that were very helpful to me in my ministry. Father Matthew was the first to encourage my writing of this book. For many years God used this priest, as His instrument of healing. I was privileged to pray over Father Matthew shortly before he went home to be with the Lord and I am sure that this holy servant of God continues to pray for all of us.

My laying on hands and praying over others first began when Father Seweryn Koszyk, allowed me to pray over the people at his church in Niagara Falls, New York. Father was a catalyst for several Marian prayer groups in the Buffalo - Niagara Falls area. He has great devotion to Our Lady. I believe that one of Father's gifts is the "gift of prayer", which he passes on to those faithful who attend his cenacles, prayer meetings and other devotions at St. George's Church, where Father Seweryn is the pastor. This parish is small in stature but a giant in prayer, especially the Rosary. I am grateful for the inspirational teachings on the Roman Catholic Church, given by this priest, in his homilies.

Father Bob Rezac, a Consolata missionary Father and a brother in Christ, whom I feel privileged to call my friend, was with me at the healing service in Medjugorje, when revelation was given regarding my being used as an instrument of healing. Before his assignment to Kenya, East Africa, Father Bob led a Marian prayer group of 120 or so people in the chapel of the Franciscan Missionary Sisters of the Divine Child Convent, located in Williamsville, New York. Father and I have had many discussions regarding prayer, our Roman Catholic faith and our mutual devotion to the Blessed Mother. I thank Father Bob for his support of my ministry. He is currently Superior of the Consolata Mission House in Williamsville, New York.

Father Bill McCarthy of "My Father's House" ministry in Connecticut was conducting a mission at Our Lady of the

Blessed Sacrament Church in Depew, New York. At the conclusion of the evening, prior to the last day of mission, I approached Father Bill, introduced myself and spoke to him of my ministry. He then invited me to join him for a cup of coffee in the rectory. Suddenly, as we were conversing, he stopped abruptly, placed his hands on my head and said "My son, continue the mission for which you have been chosen". Father Bill had received further confirmation of my commission to the healing ministry. On the last night of the church mission, Father McCarthy invited me to join him at the altar, in praying over those who had come seeking healing. I pray that the Lord continues to bless Father Bill and the beautiful works of "My Father's House" ministry.

Monsignor George Yiengst, the pastor of St. Pius X Church in Getzville, New York has allowed me to conduct healing services at his parish, for a period now of over 10 years. These monthly services consist of confession, the recitation of the Holy Rosary, the Holy Sacrifice of the Mass and finally the laying on of hands for healing of mind, body and spirit and for the gifts of the Holy Spirit, according to the Divine Will of God.

During these years, there has been television coverage, including two news specials and a feature story of the healing ministry at St. Pius X Church. On each occasion, prior to the television interviews, I approached Monsignor asking if he felt that this media coverage would benefit Our Lord, Our Lady and the Church. Without hesitation and with total trust, Monsignor gave his approval for each television airing. This television exposure of the ministry, which included testimonies of reported healings, proved to be fruitful, giving glory to God and hope to many, while increasing the number of people attending the healing services, including those at other churches.

The members of my ministry and I can never thank Monsignor Yiengst enough for his support and guidance. When Monsignor George returns home to Our Lord, I am sure that he will be greeted by - "Well done, My good and faithful servant".

Father Bill O'Brien, a former pastor of Our Lady of Lebanon Church in Niagara Falls, New York and former superior at Niagara University has been instrumental in the works surrounding my ministry from the beginning. He has celebrated many of our masses and has always been there for us. He is a true friend of this ministry and we appreciate all he has done for us. Father Bill is now serving as pastor of St. Joseph Church in Emmitsburg, Maryland and also serves as the Executive Director of Our Lady of the Angels Association and Director of the Central Association of the Miraculous Medal.

Father Alfred R. Pehrsson, a Vincentian priest, whom I have known for over 25 years, often tells this story:

"I have a rosary, blessed in Medjugorje by Our Lady. Upon returning home from pilgrimage I showed the rosary to a local prayer group. A young mother and father had been deeply concerned regarding their 4 year old son who was suffering from alopecia areata, a loss of body hair. The parents had taken the child to several area physicians seeking a medical solution for this affliction. The prognosis was that there was no cure. The child wore a baseball cap to cover his bald head. The parents who attended the prayer group asked if they could borrow the rosary that was blessed by the Mother of God. I was happy to do so. The boys parents prayed this rosary faithfully every night. Shortly , thereafter, blonde hair began to appear on the child's bald head. The end result was that the boys original full head of thick, black hair was restored and that he was able to begin school, without wearing the baseball cap to cover his former affliction."

Suffice to say that Fathers words have special meaning for me, as I am a direct witness to this story.

We thank you Mary for interceding before your Divine Son, Jesus in this situation.

Some 20 years or so ago, I recall that on one occasion, after a home mass, Father and I prayed over two women, one was healed of glaucoma and the other was cured of a hearing impairment. That was my first experience of God's healing power.

Father Al is a former pastor of Our Lady of Lebanon Church in Niagara Falls, New York. He is also a former pastor of St. Joseph Church, Emmitsburg, Maryland. I am a better person for knowing this priest.

(788) 8/19/94

My priests, My faithful priests, will be given all that is needed to shepherd My remnant flock in these, the last days. Let My faithful remnant take heart, for I will cover them with My Precious Blood, which I shed on Calvary.

(920) 5/6/95

Listen to the words of all My priest sons. They are words from Me, in spite of their faults. I minister to My faithful through these sons of whom I have chosen; therefore, support them in all things and most of all, pray for them. They will be judged as will you, except more severely, as they are the shepherds of My flocks.

Saint Maria Faustina

"O my Jesus, I beg You on behalf of the whole Church: Grant it love and the light of Your Spirit, and give power to the words of priests so that hardened hearts might be brought to repentance and return to You, O Lord. Lord, give us holy priests; You yourself maintain them in holiness. O Divine and Great High Priest, may the power of Your mercy accompany them everywhere and protect them from the devil's traps and snares which are continually being set for the souls of priests. May the power of Your mercy, O Lord, shatter and bring to naught all that might tarnish the sanctity of priests, for You can do all things." (Diary, 1052)

Rev. Seweryn Koszyk with the Holy Father Pope John Paul II

Rev. Robert Rezac

Rev. Alfred Pehrsson

Rev. William O'Brien

Rev. Matthew Swizdor

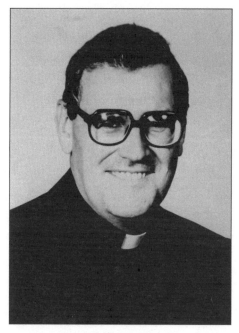

Rev. Bill McCarthy

THE LITTLE CHURCH

I have had the privilege of worshiping at a small church called St. George Roman Catholic Church in Niagara Falls, New York for some 12 years. The pastor of this parish has consecrated the parish to the Sacred Heart of Jesus and to the Immaculate Heart of Mary. This priest has a profound devotion to Our Lady and many masses (other than weekend masses) are celebrated with confessions being heard, the recitation of the Holy Rosary and other devotions, including the exposition of the Blessed Sacrament. I received many messages from Jesus and Mary during adoration at this church. This is where the Lord told me that I was to write this book. This, also, is where I first laid hands on God's people, in a church, following mass.

Here are some of the messages I received from Jesus and Mary while adoring Jesus in His Eucharistic presence:

(188) 6/27/92

After these precious moments with you and the others, My Heart is bursting with joy. I will bless this church because of the devotion to My Sacred Heart and to the Immaculate Heart of My Mother. You will know that it is I, your God, who comes to you in these times. Let My message through My Holy Mother permeate your hearts, so that you will continue to spread My words to others.

The Queen of Peace will be with you at the moments that you need her the most. She covers her little ones with her mantle of love and protects all of you from the darts of the evil one. Beware of the world and the emptiness that it holds for you.

(193-194) 7/7/92

My nucleus of "prayer warriors" pleases Me very much. They will be power and might as I am power and might. I am gathering the people who have been faithful. Pray for priests. The stray sheep will include many of them.

(197) 7/9/92

This place of worship shall become holy ground. It shall become a sanctuary for many. The Lord, your God, has placed His seal of holiness upon it. The prayers rising from this parish have reached the heavens and is pleasing as incense to the Father Almighty. Blessed be those who come within these walls. My heart cries out to the many others to follow the ways of these, My faithful. If only you knew what it means to Me, to be with you, My little remnant group.

(198) 7/9/92

I call upon you, My faithful, to plant the seeds of Me, into the hearts of the others who do not know Me as they should. Leave this holy place and tell them of Me, and of My Holy Mother and I will bless your endeavors. I call you to be My apostles of this day. I send you out to spread My word as I sent out My apostles of old. You will touch hearts as you tell them of My love for them. Invite them to spend Holy Hours with Me and My Mother. Then will I draw them deeper into My Sacred Heart and into the Immaculate Heart of My Mother.

(199) 7/9/92

Know that I use My people, My chosen ones, to reach out to the lost, the forgotten and the ones most difficult to reach. I will be with you, in prayer, in all that you do, and mostly, I will be with you, in love. My peace I give to you, which is not the peace given by the world, but it is the peace of grace and holiness of the Heavenly Father.

(203-204) 7/14/92

You come to Me and pray. You honor Me with your sincerity. I will bless you for this. I will call upon My Kingdom of Angels and Saints to intercede for you in all your needs and desires. If you call upon My Name in your moments of trouble, I will be there. If you call upon My Mother, She will filter your prayers to Me and I will call upon the Father to extend His mighty hand to protect you, and the Holy Spirit will be instilled in you for the uplifting and enlightenment of your souls.

(205) 7/14/92

Only My little ones, who come to pray in this little church are persevering to lessen My pain by their prayers and sacrifices. The world has become a cesspool of sin, but the sweetness of your prayers and companionship have pleased Me; therefore, be aware, as I send you signs of My love.

(209-210) 7/17/92

I have ordained this priest in love, from the very beginning. I have anointed his lips for the words I wish to say through him. He is a beacon in this sea of chaos, in this world today. He has stepped out in faith in areas where others would not dare to venture. He is my priest of these times. I will be with him because of his loyalty and boldness to persevere in My Name and for his devotion to My Holy Mother. His church will be anointed also, and those who attend will receive special graces when they come in an attitude of prayer and reverence to My Sacred Heart and the Immaculate Heart of My Mother.

(211-212) 7/20/92

I call for a new devotion in this church. Twenty days of exposition of My Blessed Presence and the daily reception of My Body and Blood. Many souls will be saved by this special devotion. I call upon you, My people, for it is the remnant body of My Church who will save the lost. Your sacrifice will be noted by the Heavenly Father and special graces will be bestowed upon you.

Our Lady

The healing power of my Son Jesus will descend upon His people and the light of His Presence will be seen. The flame of my Heart will warm the hearts of all who come to adore my Son, exposed to all, in the Blessed Sacrament.

Jesus

On the last day, you My son, will lay hands upon My people and pray for their well being, especially to heal their sick souls. If you believe that I am the Son of God, they will be healed.

(213) 7/20/02

Let My Heart and the Heart of My Mother, be joined to the hearts of My faithful, who persevere to visit Me, here, in this house of worship. I urge you also to bind and rebuke the evil one, as he attempts to thwart those of you who pray. Therefore, call upon My Name and seek protection beneath the mantle of My Holy Mother.

(215) 7/26/92

Many events will take place as you pray with devotion to My Sacred Heart.

(223-224) 8/5/92

I shall direct you at the proper time, for now, pray, fast and be anxious for nothing. You cannot fathom what I have in store for you and the disciples who attend and pray with fervor in this church. The Spirit will weigh heavy on that night and the faith of many will increase. It is because of your prayers and the prayers of the faithful that I want to display My presence among you.

The believers are so few, that I must manifest myself to all that I am the God of the Living, that I am universal and that I have come to save. My presence will touch hearts, so that they may believe and the hard-hearted will understand the meaning of eternal life. Those who have no god or the god of this world will know that "I AM, WHO AM". The days grow short; therefore, I must do that which will bring them to belief. I will be with you and My priest; therefore, there will be no need for anxiety. Leave all in My Hands. Be the clay and allow Me to be the Potter. Be open and ready and I will call upon you as the vessels of My works. Let the peace of My Mother bring you the peace of Me!

(225-226) 8/7/92

These twenty days will be a testimony to others. Those who persist will receive great graces. I will be among them as they pray. I will join My Heart to their hearts. These moments will turn into joyful moments for these, the faithful. Pray that evil will not pervade so that My directions will be followed in its entirety. You must proceed in faith. Worry not of failures, for I am the God of Miracles, am I not? My Will, will be done...not yours!

Be pleased that I have chosen you, and this church, to manifest Myself and to make them aware that I am the Living God. Seek not to change what I have willed, but continue as instructed in its entirety. I

45

need those to step out in faith, so that My plans may be fulfilled. Go in the knowledge that I will be with you in peace and in love!

(231) 8/12/92

These almost twenty days have refreshed Me in knowing that I have a "People of Praise" who come to spend these Holy Hours with Me and My Mother. Be at peace, be at prayer and know that your God is with you!

(233) 8/13/92

See Father and speak to him and tell him the realm of heaven will come to St. George, this "haven of prayer" and adoration in honor of My Sacred Heart.

It is the sincere prayers of this little group that brings gladness to My Heart. My Mother smiles as they enter this church each night and kneel before Me.

(235-236) 8/14/92

I have come for change. A change in the hearts of people. Change means commitment and the complacent ones are content, or seem to be content, where they are at this time in their lives. It is a false happiness because it is the happiness of this world. My world offers eternal life, while this world will pass away. I look into hearts and I do not see Me there and this brings Me sadness. I wish to be always close to My people, but they draw further away from Me. I want to save them, but they do not want salvation. Therefore My little ones, pray for them, as My prime desire is to save souls. It was for this purpose that I became man and came into this world, through My Blessed Mother. It was for their purpose that I died on the Cross.

I count on your prayers, My little flock, for their

ears are blocked and their eyes are covered and do not hear Me or see Me. This church will become a bastion of prayer and My protection will shield it against all adversaries. The gates of hell will not prevail against it. Pray over My people and let the power of My Holy Spirit come down upon them. Peace!

(238) 8/16/92

You, Father and the faithful of St. George's please Me and My Mother and We have made a resting place of this parish for Us, as well as for My people.

If only others would see that only through My Sacred Heart may they obtain the peace that they are always pursuing. Continue adoration, continue Eucharistic celebration, and continue the laying on of your hands upon My people, who come to this sanctuary of peace. Know that when you lay hands upon them, My hands and the hands of My Mother are imposed upon them, also.

The faith of My people of St. George's church, My little remnant body, will continue to soar and souls will be brought into the Kingdom by their stalwart prayers.

(242) 8/19/92

The people of St. George are dear to Me and that is why I call them to continuous prayer. Not many are committed to the life of prayer. They will be compensated as they pass through the doors of this parish. Their endeavors and their good works will not go unnoticed by Me and My Mother. As for you My son, tell My priest to carry on as he is, with the Holy Hours and you lay your hands gently upon them, that My glory may be witnessed by all. Stay, My son, in deep prayer, continuously, and I will bless the work that I have prepared for you. Go in peace!

(243) 8/20/92

The church of St. George will share in the grace and benefits, as this congregation increases in faith.

(246) 8/21/92

The people of St. George, the faithful, will hear Me speaking through My anointed priest. His words are those that I want conveyed to you. Pray fervently, My little flock, to compensate for those who do not pray or for those who pray little. The power of your prayers enter into My Kingdom and My Angels and Saints rejoice as they hear your voices.

(259) 8/30/92

Be examples, dear children, to all the others, so that they may see conversion as the way to My eternal Kingdom.

(262) 8/31/92

Our Lady

My son, as you pray over them, give the glory, always, to my Son who has given all to you and to His people. I will never leave you. I will always be Mother to my faithful, here, in this "little parish of love and faith".

(316) 10/3/92

All will come to pass, as I have foretold. My people of St. George will experience an event, which will bring blessings upon them. They shall know that I, their God, love them and convey My love through the Immaculate Heart of My Mother. I give them My Holy Peace, as I give My peace to you.

(331) 10/12/92

My power shall come upon this edifice of worship and they will marvel at the manifestations which will be displayed. Look to the near future. Look to Me. Look to My Mother. Pray, fast, love!

(339) 10/16/92

Days will come of which hardships will befall the "little church", but because of My love, all problems will be overcome. Stand firm in faith, My people, for none can topple My "little parish of holiness". My Glory will emerge from this church, as I bestow My blessing upon it, and My "people of continuous prayer". There will shortly be a renewal of faith, as I intercede in the events to come.

(357-358) 10/29/92

Our Lady

You will see me soon my son. My priest son will see me, too. All those who pray in earnest to my Immaculate Heart will view my radiance as I come before them. All will come to pass, at a time least expected by any.

Jesus

Tell all to keep My commandments. Tell all to pray, to fast, to confess their sins, to hold Me always in adoration, and mostly, to receive Me in My Eucharistic form. My presence will be among you, as you come before Me in prayer and in adoration of My Eucharistic body in My "little church of holiness". My peace and My love go out to My people, the remnant flock who persevere for My sake.

(361) 11/1/92

My "poor church" will be exalted, not because of earthly riches, but because of the prayers of My "little ones" that have reached the heavens. These are the poor who have become wealthy by their prayers, unlike the rich who have become poor by their lack of faith and their avoidance of Me and My Mother.

(364) 11/5/92

Father is gifted and will see My Mother, you will too. Let not the words of others dissuade you, keep your eyes on the Trinity and on My Mother. All will come to pass in My time. You will be engaged in the saving work of souls as you introduce them to My Kingdom, by way of this ministry. They will be converted by Me and to Me, through you, as you pray over them and invoke My Name.

(372-373) 11/9/92

My people of the "little parish" will not be undermined by the few who look to themselves and not to Me. My priest wants prayer and not controversy. The glory is to be mine and I will not give way to others. I will bless those who seek Me and I will shun those who come as the Pharisees of My time. My priest will not be led astray as his eyes are upon Me and the "Woman clothed in the Sun". Woe to those who attempt to covet My glory. Be meek, I say to them, lest My anger be activated. I came to this church to bring peace among this "little flock". I will not tolerate those who would bring disorder and confusion in order to elevate themselves, as in the manner of the world.

(381) 11/19/92

Our Lady

I will come to you at a time least expected. The experience of which will be enlightening and pleasing to all that view my presence. The prayers of the faithful who support the salvation of souls is what brings me to you in the midst of chaos in this world of iniquity and opposition to my Son, Jesus. His justice will prevail and those of whom have ignored Him and His precepts will know themselves in their sins and repent, some in sorrow, many in fear. There will be many others that will come to know Him, before this time of "Divine Justice".

(388) 11/26/92

You have said you sense that something special will occur in this place of worship. Something has already occurred and more will ensue. Continue the prayers, the fasting and offer to Me any sufferings that come upon you, My priest and My people.

(390-391) 11/26/92

I have given him My Wisdom and he speaks anointed words, in My Name. He is among the minority of this world, but is major in My Kingdom. His service will be the shepherding of "remnant groups". These groups will not be known for their numbers, but by their witness for Me.

He has planted many seeds of which few have taken root, but it is as written, "many are called, few are chosen". Let My Spirit fall upon My chosen priest and protect him, as he goes forward, without hesitation, to do battle for Me and My commandments.

I am the Way, the Truth and the Life; no one goes to the Father except by Me. Know also, that through My Mother, many will find Me for I have appointed

Her as My Ambassador of Conversion. Be always at peace, My little son, and be peace to others, as I am peace to you.

(395-396) 12/1/92

Relate to Father to continue to feed My flock and prepare them for My Coming. I am preceded by My Heavenly Messenger who toils diligently to save the stray before the "time of grace" expires. She has been sent to replace those of My shepherds who have led My flock in error. Pray for My shepherds that they may return to the path of true faith, as I have ordained it to be.

Our Lady

Listen always to my Son, even though it seems other than you would want it to be. His is the Knowledge and Wisdom from the Father and all else matters not. Be not anxious as all things are made good for those who believe with a humble heart. Know that I will be with you in your times of trial to see you through. Put any fretfulness behind you and relax beneath my Holy Mantle. Concentrate on the work designed for you by us. This will be the means of conversion for many. I will be praying with you, as we petition for the needs of those seeking aid. My Son will be the giver of gifts, graces and healings, according to His Divine Will.

(409) 12/20/92

I will send signs to St. George, the church of little recognition, so that it will be known as My "chosen church".

(444) 2/3/93

I have already shown you, My priest son and others signs of the presence of My Mother and I. Continue to pray, fast and address Me in My Holy Presence on the altar. Know without any doubt that I am working to bring about what is needed to enhance the belief of many, by the utilization of My "little church".

(454-455) 2/17/93

My Mother will appear. All of My remnant flock will bow to her majestic aura. She will come amidst the people as they adore Me in My Eucharistic splendor. Let My priest son know that I am with him as he carries My precepts to all the faithful.

(519-520) 5/2/93

Be patient, concentrate on your mission, of which you have been commissioned for your life's work. The church of St. George will soon be known to all. I will manifest myself through My Holy Mother; She, who is the Queen of Heaven and of all men and of all angels. Signs will be given from above and all doubts will disappear. Cling to the Gospel, the Sacraments and My Commandments. Align yourself with the tenets of the Holy Father, he who was chosen by My Mother. Be bold as you lay your hands on My people, invoke My Holy Spirit, call upon My Mother to pray with you and give of your love and compassion to all who come seeking "new life". You will pray, I will heal as needed, according to My Divine Will. Go, wherever I send you, as your mission will take you in places not thought of by you. This is your course. Follow my direction. Come often to Me for this direction. You walk in My protection. Peace, My little son.

(529-530) 05/13/93

Our Lady

St. George will withstand the attacks as he did the dragon of old. I will be among my people in a way that cannot be denied. Let the prayers and devotions continue, as these examples please us and are witness to others. Pay no heed to persecution as the evil one attempts to thwart the endeavors of my little ones of the remnant flock. Change no course at this time, but follow the path of these messages.

Let my persistent priest, whom we have chosen, continue to shepherd my people in worship of my Son and all will find peace in the "Garden of my Immaculate Heart".

(531) 5/13/93

You will be gifted further, with Wisdom and Knowledge, as I have foretold. You have been chosen to follow the example of a holy priest; therefore, you will be blessed in ministry. Keep your eyes on Me, stay united to My Holy Mother and allow My power to work through you to bring honor and glory to Me.

(535) 5/19/93

Do as you are, My son, as all will come to fruition according to My Divine Will. Know that the others who sacrifice with their prayers and infirmities, will gain favor in My Heavenly Kingdom. Their devotion to My Mother and to Me will bring salvation to them and to their families. It is these of whom I speak, the remnant body of believers who will persevere to the end. Be united to this flock, as you are to the other remnant flocks.

(537-539) 5/21/93

Listen to the silence. You will find Me there. Call upon My Mother now and she will reveal herself to you.

Our Lady

My little son, my place in this church is among my faithful flock, the remnant that gathers daily within the confines of these walls. It is because of them that souls are being saved. They number among the few faithful in the remnant flocks around the globe. I call upon them for continued prayer and adoration to my Son, Jesus, for it is the only way to lessen that which is to come upon this earth. Know too, my little ones, that I will sustain you in all your trials and will be with you in times of darkness. I cannot help those who will not give up the material resources of this world in favor of the spiritual blessings of my Son. Look to me for guidance, look to me for example and look to me for a love that the world cannot offer you. You please me, my children, as you come in adoration before my Son, the one who gave His life, that you may have life.

I will come to you, to each of you, as you pray your "Ave Marias" to me. Let my motherly arms enfold you each time you come before me in reverence. See me in your daily chores and endeavors, for I will be but a breathe away, watching over you. I give to each and everyone of you, my love and my peace, as does my Son, Jesus.

(544) 5/26/93

Life Offering

Many souls were healed through the prayers of the faithful and by your obedience to My wishes. These were conversions, deepening of faith and the general well being of all who attended.

Let My Spirit continue to manifest, as you lay your hands upon My people. This will be new beginnings for the evangelization of My Church, My true Church. Let all who come be blessed in the Name of the Father, and of the Son and of the Holy Spirit.

(545) 5/27/93

Let My Spirit come upon each of you and give you the desires of your hearts, if they conform with the means of salvation of your souls.

(569) 6/25/93

Our Lady

Let it be known to you that I love you for your devotion to me and for your faithfulness to my Son. On this special day, I bless each and every one of you and know, also, that those who remain to the end, will be with me in the triumphant reign of my Immaculate Heart and in the supreme reign of my Son in the New Terrestrial Paradise. My peace to you, my little ones.

(573) 6/30/93

This church, My son, will soon be uplifted, as I send My Spirit down upon it by means of My Holy Messenger, My Mother. She will spread My rays of light throughout the "little church of prayer".

(577) 7/8/93

This is the church I favor for it bears the sign of holiness. The prayers forthcoming from within its walls are as pleasing incense to Me.

(622) 9/15/93

Our Lady

Lean on me, my little son, and let all your cares be transferred to me. Come within the garden of my Immaculate Heart and find refuge there. I can transpose all burdens to joy. There will be the time for sadness, but also, there will be the time of happiness. Be rooted in the precepts of my Son. Be obedient to my Son. Persevere for my Son. St. George will persevere, for I have put purpose in it's being. Continue prayers and allow the Spirit of my Son to work within its walls. Search the scriptures for confirmation of my words. Be fervent in the works I call you to and be obedient to my teaching, lest you stray.

(630) 9/25/93

I cannot tell you what it means to Me to find this little gathering of My faithful here at this place. Your number are few, but your prayers are powerful before My Heavenly Throne. Continue to honor Me and My Mother and I will greet all of you at the door of My Kingdom.

(640-641) 10/11/93

My priest son of the "little church" continues to please Me with his perseverance in the true precepts of My church. His suffering is not in vain, as many souls have been salvaged from the road to perdition because of his unending loyalty and love for his God and My Mother. Relate to him that Our peace and Our love goes wherever he goes.

(651) 10/30/93

Our Lady

This holy church shall be blessed by my presence. I

will come as the mother of all. Your prayers have been my invitation and I come to all who would receive me in their hearts.

(660) 11/27/93

This church will go on as an example to others. Although, few in number, the prayers emanating from these pews are sincere and are pleasing to Us. Many souls have been assisted by these faithful of My "little church". Peace to all of you, My children.

(689) 1/29/94

Our Lady

It is my sincere wish to come to this little abode of my Son, Jesus. I wish to catapult this "house of prayer" to a place of worship and conversion. It is the prayers of these faithful few that gain favor with my Son. Therefore, be prepared for I will come when it will be least expected.

(706) 3/4/94

Listen to the pounding of nails into My hands.

(707) 3/5/94

My brilliance shines through to all of you before Me, as I reveal My Eucharistic Presence in this place.

(715) 3/17/94

Our Lady

I will be coming soon. The tears will flow from my eyes. You will feel my presence among you. You will smell my presence among you. You will know that I, your Heavenly Mother, is here among you.

(724) 4/4/94

Yes, they are My people, My faithful remnant, and it pleases Me so to see them here keeping company with Me and praying to My Sacred Heart. My Mother and I know that this ending "time of mercy" will leave many short of the Kingdom. But, I will extend My hand to them, so that they may not find their way to perdition.

(740) 5/6/94

Our Lady

My little church of the faithful ones: I will watch over each and every one of you. An event will take place that will open hearts to the happenings of these final times. Eyes will be opened and some will see, for the first time, that the Kingdom of God is close at hand. Still others will remain with their blindfolds intact. Pray, pray for those who cannot find their way so that a light will shine on the path to conversion and salvation.

(798) 9/5/94

This little church which speaks of My love is a beacon in this sea of darkness, which is called earth. I have given it My seal of Holiness and My Divine Blessings, in response to the many prayers and sacrifices so amply given by this very little remnant. Be of assurance that My Holy Mother is among you, this night and every night that you give reverence to Me, in My Presence, on this altar. Continue to seek Me for all your needs and I will continue to extend, to you, all the gifts and graces necessary for salvation in eternal life. Remain My children in the Name of the Father, and of the Son and of the Holy Spirit.

(801) 9/10/94

Our Lady

My children come to me daily, and proclaim their love for me. However, if their actions do not conform to their words, then they are not following My Son's ways. Therefore, transform, you who have not listened to My messages ...

(802) 9/11/94

Our Lady

...and learn to lean on Him, who has redeemed you at the terrible price. He will be your solace and your protector, if only you will let Him be the center of your life.

Somehow I knew, when each message given to me was completed. I also knew whether it was Jesus or Mary speaking to my heart.

I HAVE NO WORDS OF EXPLANATION FOR THIS!!!

HIS HEALING PEACE

"And God's peace, which is far beyond human under-standing, will keep your hearts and minds safe in union with Christ Jesus". (Philippians 4:7)

I have come to know the meaning of the above scripture passage, as I pray over God's people. It is not the surface peace one can obtain by activity or inactivity. It is the peace from within, which may be given only by our Lord, Jesus Christ. The following examples serve as a few illustrations of God's healing peace:

A young child with a rare disease was fussing and crying as I laid hands upon her. In probably a minute or so, she stopped crying, calmed down and seemed to be completely at peace. Moreover, her baby brother, being held by his grandmother across the room, had been constantly crying. As I ceased praying, he had stopped crying and was fast asleep. A coincidence maybe, but I would like to believe that this was the working of the Holy Spirit in that room and in those children.

While praying over three sisters in a private home, there was also a ten-year-old nephew of one of the ladies present. I observed him praying as I laid hands on each of the women and then asked if I might pray over him. I began praying and he rested in God's Holy Spirit. While lying on the floor in this form of ecstasy, he began shaking and one of those in my ministry who was kneeling near his head said that she heard his teeth chattering. He soon stopped shaking, sat up and related to us what he had seen: "I was standing by a lake and I was very cold. Then a beautiful lady came out from the lake, came over and kissed me on my cheek and then I felt a warm peace all over. The lady was wearing a blue gown and had a crown of stars on her head. I have never seen such a beautiful face."

Needless to say, we each drew our own conclusion as to who the child had seen, Mary, the Mother of God.

I had prayed over a woman who had just been diagnosed with breast cancer and was going through extreme fear and anxiety. She rested in God's Holy Spirit and when she arose, all fear and anxiety were gone and said that she was now able to accept the Lord's will, in her infirmity. It appeared that the peace of Christ had permeated her entire being.

While praying over an elderly woman with a terminal disease, her face suddenly became aglow with a peaceful smile. When she opened her eyes, we learned that a vision of Our Lady had been given to her.

In praying for others and inquiring how they feel after being prayed over, the most frequent response is that they feel a deep sense of peace. Some say they feel relaxed others that they are calmer and still others use the words, tranquil or serene. I believe the bottom line is that they have received from Jesus some measure of peace. Peace is what we are all seeking, because with His peace "the peace that transcends all understanding", we can cope in all trials, whether they be spiritual, physical or emotional. It is Jesus Christ, and He only, who administers this kind of inner peace, and we must realize that this peace is a gift from the Holy Spirit.

One of the words most often used by Our Lady, in her messages coming from Medjugorje, is PEACE. After much prayerful meditation and after seeing how Our Lord freely gives of His holy peace to His people, my ministry has adopted the name "Queen of Peace Healing Ministry". However, looking back on the following message, I discovered that the Lord had already given the name to this ministry:

(69) 9/18/91

Cling to My Holy Mother, for she is the "Queen of Peace". Allow her to penetrate your heart, so that you may have a more intimate relationship with her.

God wants us to have His beautiful gift of inner peace. We have but to open our hearts to the Holy Spirit and He will pour into our hearts, His graces and blessings.

(264) 9/1/92

You have told others of the word, "peace". You were right. This word encompasses all that the world strives for, but most do not know how to attain it because they think that they will find peace in things and places. The only "true peace" is Me. When My people find Me, they find peace and then conversion has taken place. Even those who have converted must continue to seek Me in an unending search for the final peace which is eternal life in My Kingdom.

(459) 2/21/93

As time goes on, you will learn more and more the meaning of the word "peace". It is through this word that My Mother speaks to My people. If they listen to Her messages, then peace will reign in their hearts.

A child is born to us!
A son is given to us!
And he will be our ruler.
He will be called, "Wonderful"
"Counselor"
"Mighty God"
"Eternal Father"
*"**Prince of Peace**". (Isaiah 9:6)*

MARY, QUEEN OF PEACE

I believe that it was Mary, mother of Jesus, the God-Man, who was instrumental in my being commissioned to perform the works for which I have been chosen. I have had a devotion to Our Lady since my childhood when I attended novenas to Our Lady of the Miraculous Medal. Some have said that Our Lady is not often mentioned in the Bible. This is true; however, when scripture did speak of Mary it was highly significant:

> *"I will make you and <u>the woman</u> hate each other; her offspring and yours will always be enemies. <u>Her offspring will crush your head</u>, and you will bite their heel". (Genesis 3:15).*

> *"When Elizabeth heard Mary's greeting, the baby moved within her. Elizabeth was filled with the Holy Spirit and said in a loud voice, '<u>You are the most blessed of all women, and blessed is the child you will bear! Why should this great thing happen to me, that my Lord's mother comes to visit me?</u> For as soon as I heard your greeting, the baby within me jumped with gladness. How happy you are to believe that the Lord's message to you will come true!" (Luke 1:41-45).*

At the wedding in Cana, in Galilee, where Jesus performed His first public miracle by changing water into wine, Mary was present.

> *"Standing close to Jesus' cross were his mother, his mother's sister, Mary the wife of Clopas, and Mary Magdalene. Jesus saw his mother and the disciple he loved standing there; so he said to his mother, "<u>He is your son</u>". Then he said to the disciple, <u>She is your mother:</u>" From that time the disciple took her to live in his home." (John 19:25-27).*

Then a great and mysterious sight appeared in the sky.
<u>*There was a woman, whose dress was the sun and who*</u>
<u>*had the moon under her feet and a crown of twelve*</u>
<u>*stars on her head.*</u> *She was soon to give birth, and the*
pains and suffering of childbirth made her cry out.
Another mysterious sight appeared in the sky. There was
a huge red dragon with seven heads and ten horns and
a crown on each of his heads. With his tail he dragged
a third of the stars out of the sky and threw them down
to the earth. He stood in front of the woman, in order to
eat her child as soon as it was born. <u>*Then she gave*</u>
<u>*birth to a son, who will rule over all nations*</u> *with an*
iron rod. But the child was snatched away and taken to
God and his throne." (Rev. 12:1-5)

(84) 10/20/91

**Lean heavily on the words of My Holy Mother, for
she will lead you in what I have planned.**

(88-89) 10/26/91

Our Lady

**Let it be known that I come to you as your spiritual
Mother. I have come into the world to bring peace.
Not many listen to me, but I keep calling for
responses. The children of my Son will hear me and
others will not. I pray for conversions for all sinners.
I am your Mother and I love you, as your mother
loved you.**

(101-102) 11/28/91

Our Lady

**Continue to pray and be in the will of my Son for it
is He who will show you the way to holiness. I will be
there to guide you and console you in times of need.**

(130) 2/12/92

Our Lady

Seek Him continuously for Wisdom and Knowledge and His will, which will be done through you. Look to His Spirit and He will lead you to the salvation of many souls.

(167) 5/10/92

Our Lady

I came to you in Medjugorje, I can come to you here. I am where my Son is, we are always together. I pray with you as you pray to my Son.

(181) 6/7/92

Call upon My Holy Mother at every opportunity, for she is the guide of these times. Listen to her voice, as she speaks to you, for her words are My words.

(189) 6/27/92

Our Lady

Remain in the garden of my Immaculate Heart, for there you will find comfort and peace.

(265) 7/14/92

Our Lady

My Son wishes to bestow upon His people, all the graces and gifts, so that they may be fortified for the times which are to come. They have but to open their hearts, receive and believe that it is Jesus who is the giver of all gifts. Let them be steadfast in prayer, fasting and sacrifice and the Kingdom of Heaven will be theirs.

(211-212) 7/20/92

Our Lady

The healing power of my Son, Jesus, will descend upon His people and the light of His presence will be seen. The flame of my Heart will warm the hearts of all who come to adore my Son, exposed to all in the Blessed Sacrament.

(230) 8/11/92

My Mother will be at your side.

(285-286) 9/15/92

Our Lady

My little son, new events will transpire as you allow my Son to lead you in this ministry. This was foretold to you, but you were dubious. My Son uses whomever He chooses. As Savior of the world, this is His privilege.

Be content that you are among the chosen for much more awaits you in the works of love to be accomplished for the glory of my Son. I will pray with you, as you pray over them, therefore, it will always be when two or more are gathered in His Name.

(320) 10/6/92

Our Lady

My Son does not speak in haste. This ministry was decided long ago. He has allowed me to assist you, as you have honored me with your prayers and reverence. I will be with you as you pray for my children, as you lay your hands upon them and as you call on my Son to heal them of their afflictions.

(330-331) 10/12/92

Our Lady

Through my words, my little son, you will entertain thoughts of furtherance of the ministry. You will be led to other places and will impose your hands on other people. My Son will direct and glean you as He wills. The time is running out. The harvest must be completed. There are but few hands to assist in this task.

(461-463) 2/22/93

Our Lady

My little son, be pleased that my Jesus has chosen you to be a standard bearer for the cause of conversion. Through this ministry and other means, will your service to our God, my Son, be accomplished. Keep your eyes upon my Son, let Him be your inspiration, your source of strength, and your protection. Only in this way can you persevere in these, the final days. We will lay hands upon them, together, and the power of the Holy Spirit will come down to fill them and to heal them of whatever afflictions they have, according to the Divine Will of my Son. Pray over them on any and all occasions, as you are commissioned by Jesus to do. The time when I am to appear will be at the discretion of my Son. It will be when it is needed most. More prayer, more fasting is needed everywhere: in the church, in the home, in the workplace. Only the chosen few pray with the heart. The others succumb to the prayer of duty or to the prayer of tepidity. Come visit me often. Speak to me. We are prayer partners, you and I. We must intercede for those who are sad, hurting and especially for those who are seeking conversion and do not know how to convert. My son, you were not chosen by chance; therefore, know that responsibility will be placed upon you regarding assistance of shepherding the flock into the fold.

(475) 3/13/93

Our Lady

It is through my Immaculate Heart that peace and conversion will be promulgated to my people. I have been sent on a mission of grace and mercy to free the captives and to release goodness into this world of iniquity. Let my messages not fall on deaf ears, but let my words penetrate hearts so that more will enter the Heavenly Paradise.

Our Lady has said many times that She is not only the Mother of Catholics, but is the Mother of all people.

Mother Mary, my desire is to know you in a more profound and intimate way and I ask that you continue to lead me to your Son, Jesus.

WORKINGS OF THE HOLY SPIRIT

There are no limitations to what our great God can do. In a television interview a reporter asked me what I feel when I pray over His people. My reply is that I feel mostly nothing, except love and compassion for their needs. But then, why would I feel anything? I am only an instrument of healing. There is but one healer and He is the one who died on the Cross for us, Jesus Christ. My laying on of hands and praying over people is likened to a tilted straw; pour liquid into one end of the straw and it comes out the other.

It is the power to heal that comes from Jesus, through me, and is poured out into those over whom I pray. They are the ones who experience various manifestations, some of which are heat, tingling sensations, visions, light, tears, words, the odor of sanctity and if it be God's Will, healing, peace and the gifts of His Holy Spirit.

ALMOST ALL RECEIVE SOME MEASURE OF INNER PEACE.

The Lord bestows upon certain people, the gifts of His Holy Spirit; however, these gifts are to be used for the edification of others.

(233) 8/13/92

The word of knowledge will flow through you My son, and you will know how to pray.

(363) 11/5/92

You will be used in many ways because of your openness and your pliability. My Blood and the mantle of My Mother will be your protection in the ministry. Pray for words of knowledge before the time of imposition of your hands upon them, perhaps throughout that very day.

Prior to each of the healing services, the Lord gives me insight of what to pray for when I lay hands on His people, including spiritual, physical and emotional afflictions. This does not, of course, limit His healing power to these particular problems. For as our God and Creator, we know that He can do all things, according to His Divine Will. Furthermore, His healing power extends to those not present at the healing service, but receiving prayer through others, as supported by Holy Scripture:

"A Roman officer there had a servant who was very dear to him; the man was sick and about to die. When the officer heard about Jesus, he sent some Jewish elders to ask him to come and heal his servant. They came to Jesus and begged him earnestly, 'This man really deserves your help. He loves our people and he himself built a synagogue for us.'

So Jesus went with them. He was not far from the house when the officer sent friends to tell him, 'Sir, don't trouble yourself. I do not deserve to have you come into my house, neither do I consider myself worthy to come to you in person. Just give the order, and my servant will get well. I, too, am a man placed under the authority of superior officers, and I have soldiers under me. I order this one, 'Go!' and he goes; I order that one, 'Come!' and he comes; and I order my slave, 'Do this!' and he does it.'

Jesus was surprised when he heard this; he turned around and said to the crowd following him, 'I tell you, I have never found faith like this, not even in Israel!'

The messengers went back to the officer's house and found his servant well." (Luke 7: 2-10)

"Then Jesus went back to Cana in Galilee, where he had turned the water into wine. A government official was there whose son was sick in Capernaum. When he heard that Jesus had come from Judea to Galilee, he went to him and asked him to go to Capernaum and

heal his son, who was about to die. Jesus said to him, 'None of you will ever believe unless you see miracles and wonders.'

'Sir,' replied the official, 'come with me before my child dies.' Jesus said to him, 'Go; your son will live!'

The man believed Jesus' words and went. On his way home his servants met him with the news, 'Your boy is going to live!'

He asked them what time it was when his son got better, and they answered, 'It was one o'clock yesterday afternoon when the fever left him.' Then the father remembered that it was at that very hour when Jesus had told him, 'Your son will live.'

So he and all his family believed." (John 4: 46-53)

"Jesus left that place and went off to the territory near the cities of Tyre and Sidon. A Canaanite woman who lived in that region came to him. 'Son of David!' she cried out. 'Have mercy on me, sir! My daughter has a demon and is in a terrible condition.'

But Jesus did not say a word to her. His disciples came to him and begged him, 'Send her away! She is following us and making all this noise!'

Then Jesus replied, 'I have been sent only to the lost sheep of the people of Israel.' At this the woman came and fell at his feet. 'Help me, sir!' she said. Jesus answered, 'It isn't right to take the children's food and throw it to the dogs.'

'That's true, sir,' she answered, 'but even the dogs eat the leftovers that fall from their master's table.' So Jesus answered her, 'You are a woman of great faith! What you want will be done for you.' And at that very moment her daughter was healed." (Matthew 15: 21-28)

CORNELIUS

While in meditation the Lord said to me:

(12) 7/28/91

"Cornelius" has a special meaning for you. It will be revealed to you at the proper time.

I put these words on a back burner and thought nothing more of it. But then, there was this time later when I was sitting in my dentist's office reading an article in a magazine and found that the author of the article was named "John J. **Cornelius**". Another time I would be driving behind a white tractor-trailer and on the rear of the vehicle, in large black letters, would be the words "**Cornelius** Trucking Company". I was sitting at a counter in a restaurant and there before me, on the nameplate of a soft drink dispenser was "**Cornelius** Manufacturing Company". While perusing the real estate transactions in the newspaper, the one transaction that seemed to stand out on the page was "Jones to **Cornelius**". Situations such as these went on for a long time. I kept thinking, "Why is the Lord calling me Cornelius"?

This sent me to Holy Scripture as I recalled in Acts, Chapter 10, the story of Peter and the Roman Centurion, Cornelius. And yet, I could not put anything together. I then went into research at the library. I read about Cornelius the poet, Cornelius the Archbishop and others. Still no answer!

Then one day, the Lord said to me:

(76) 10/6/91

Be assured that you are never alone as I have given you a Guardian Angel, yet unnamed. Name him as you wish.

It was as though someone had turned on a bright light

in a totally dark room and I knew, without a doubt, that Cornelius was the name of my Guardian Angel. In confirmation of this, a few days later someone gave me an article with the history of Blessed John Cornelius (a Cornelius who escaped me in my research), stating the day, month, and year of his beatification.

IT WAS THE EXACT DAY, MONTH AND YEAR OF MY BIRTH!

(86) 10/26/91

My Holy Mother watches over you, as always. The "Little Flower" watches over you, as does Cornelius.

(119) 1/12/92

I will be with you at all times; therefore, have no fear. Call on your guardian angel when necessary.

Cornelius is with me always and I thank God for this blessing; I know through experience that my angel has assisted me in many difficult situations. Call on your Guardian Angel to help with your problems and situations, for Jesus gives an angel to each of us, at birth to guide and protect us throughout our lives. THIS IS A SPECIAL GIFT FROM GOD!

THE TEACHING CONTINUES

During a television interview I was asked, "Why do you think you were chosen to be used as an instrument of healing?" When I first began serving God in His ministry, I asked myself the same question, but I have since arrived at this understanding; the Lord does not elect His servants because of their level of holiness or because they are perfect. If that were the case, He would not have chosen me, as I am imperfect. Prominent figures in Holy Scripture and those chosen to serve God in these latter times will bear this out.

It is my belief that this is true in the lives of others that are used in God's service in the many different ministries that exist. I thank God for using me as an instrument of His healing power, in spite of me! With that being said, His words of teaching continues:

(72-74) 9/30/91

Let the peace you felt in Medjugorje again be with you now. You will begin a new journey on the path that I will lead you. You will have help soon. Count the burdens as blessings for I, the Savior of the World, am with you.

<u>Seek Me at every opportunity for I am the answer to all things. Consult no other!</u>

I will continue to lead you, teach you, support you, as long as you remain in My Will. Be conscious of the many ways I speak to you throughout your day.

(76-77) 10/6/91

Call on Me and My Mother whenever you need help, as We are your protectors. Ask Michael to protect you also, for he is an angel of love. Live for Me, always, live for My Mother, and all will go well. The life of holiness is not an even path, but it is the only path to Me. Look to the future to do My Will in

whatever area I direct you. Question not, for My decisions are for your good and the good of others. Be open to My promptings. Pray more. Fast more. Try to lead a holy life. I need those who persevere. Leave here with the knowledge that we will be one in whatever is asked of you.

(81-84) 10/12/91

Be patient and let Me open the doors for you. It is the only way. I have chosen you, a weak vessel, so that I may show My strength.

Be at My disposal for when I call on you. Listen always to the still, soft voice for it will be Me. I cannot do for others, unless I have the co-operation of My chosen. Be humble and I will work through you. Be as a child in all spiritual matters. Let My Sacred Heart encompass you daily, in all that you do, so that you will become holy, as I am holy.

Listen closely to new revelations. Continue to seek Me for I am the center of all things. The sick will be healed, as I deem necessary, for their good.

Learn more of Me, so that the ministry will flourish.

(92-93) 11/2/91

The peace of My Mother will be with you, have I not told you so? You have learned some of My lessons — there is more to learn. You are a willing pupil.

Know the time, as you feel the Spirit alive in You. Sift the noises of confusion. Choose what is needed, dispense of the rest.

(94-95) 11/4/91

Be sure of your commitment to Me. I need the stalwart and the committed. Leave the world behind and follow Me.

I will work the miracle in your life — a life changing in service to Me.

Be Me to those whom I will send you. I will use you, as you are open. Listen, as I minister to your spirit, so that you may minister to others. Be not opposed to My Will, but be secure in the thought that it is My Will. I leave you now in the presence of My Mother.

Our Lady

Follow my Son with your obedience, for that is what is needed to fulfill your purpose in life.

(99) 11/24/91

If you seek Me, you will find Me. Look into the depths of your heart. I will be there.

(104-106) 12/7/91

You are at peace this night. It is the power of My Holy Spirit that grants you this peace. You have learned a great deal over these past several months. Would you have, if I had not brought you to your knees?

You have learned of peace, loneliness and sadness, of the poor and the lonely, the sick and the depressed. Would you have learned, if you were on the mountaintop? No, the valleys are where the lessons are found!

I can only do for you that which you will allow Me to do. Gifts are already being activated within you. Be ready for when I call upon you. I have flooded you in an ocean of peace, this is to show My presence within you.

(107-108) 12/9/91

We are together again, My son. Let the peace I have given you penetrate your every fiber. I continue to bless your efforts, as you continue to seek Me. I will see to all your needs, spiritual and temporal. You will stay in obedience to Me. Love those that are, seemingly, impossible to love.

(109-110) 12/16/91

You will know what to do when the time comes. It will be by My authority that you will speak. The words will be My words, the time, My time. I have brought you almost to a closed circle. It will be by My power that you will close the circle. I will lead you to the well; drink there of the living water which I have anointed for you.

I have left you a legacy, that which will honor Me and that which only you can fulfill. My power can only be used through an open and willing vessel. I have called you to this task. You will change, all about you will change. The work must be done. Again, I say, the time is short, the workers few. Lean on Me for all your needs. Come to Me often. Praise Me, let Me console you. You are My son, let nothing separate us.

(111-112) 12/25/91

Continue to pray and seek, I will do the rest. The why's, where's and when's come under My jurisdiction.

(113) 1/2/92

I am the still, small voice that comes within your heart. Be attuned to listening and you will hear Me.

(115) 1/2/92

Be an open vessel to receive Me and let Me be dispensed through you.

You are coming to the end of the valley. The hilltop is now in sight. This was the only way I could reach you at this time. Be patient and endure, so that I may use you without blemish.

(116) 1/2/92

Reach out to the poor in spirit. Let them know of My Spirit. Let them know of My Holy Mother. There will be a deeper anointing of your spirit, as you move in the ways of holiness. I classify the rich and the poor as equals, you do the same. All are My people, when they are aligned in My Will.

(119) 1/12/92

You come again to Me, this night for direction. I continue to give you direction, day by day, as I have previously done. Can you walk where I have walked? Can you bleed as I have bled? Be content with your cross for it is light. Your only concern is to pray and be obedient to My Holy Will.

(123-124) 1/24/92

Be committed to those who need love. You will be My Hands, My Feet, My Voice, if you choose. I will work in you and through you. Let My Spirit govern your whole being.

Seek Me as you have been seeking Me and I will bless you abundantly. Let the love I give to you spread among those you meet. You will know what to do My son, be not concerned. I have given you the key to a ministry yet untapped. Clear your mind of the things of the world and let My Kingdom reign within you, totally, and without obstruction.

(127-128) 2/12/92

Patience is a virtue and like Job, I have given you this virtue. Look not upon the burden of others for comparison, but look upon it as a grace for the salvation of others. Call to mind Abraham for his faith. This was also a grace from God. Let it be a constant reminder to you of why I died on the Cross. Was it not also to save souls? Would you do any less? Be pleased, that I ask this of you, for no greater love has one than to lay down his life for his brother. You will see My Hand everywhere and in all things. You will know that the Lord, your God, is by your side.

(132-133) 2/21/92

You will heal the sick and cast out demons, in My Name, as did My apostles of yore. I charge you with the leadership of this cause, not because you are especially qualified, but because I deem it so.

(141-142) 3/22/92

Fix your eyes upon the Host and you will know. Time has been shortened and the sick must be healed, so that My power will be known. I cannot use you if you do not have complete trust in Me. Your world has been shaken, but good will come of this. Practice the patience I have given you. Let things happen in the natural course.

I will bless you and the ministry as you go forward to do battle for me. I will deepen your prayer life as you attempt to meet Me, day by day.

(147) 4/10/92

Be cognizant of the fact that your service to Me will be for My people. They must be nurtured in love and brought into the Kingdom, as I direct.

(154) 4/18/92

Allow My Heart and My Mother's Heart to infuse you with all the graces and gifts that I wish to bestow upon you. I have claimed you for My own, therefore, no one can interfere with My plans. Stay in an attitude of prayer at all times and let My Spirit guide you.

(155) 4/27/92

Let what I have spoken to you thus far be absorbed in its entirety. I have come to you in words and now I will come to you in visions.

(157) 4/27/92

Continue to seek, continue to pray. My plans will not be thwarted for I seek to free My people through My instruments of love whom I choose.

(161) 5/3/92

I look upon you as a leader to transform My people. You cannot understand this now, but soon you will comprehend.

My covenant with you will be one of love and mutual understanding. You will know what is expected of you. You cannot fathom why or how you will be used. The reasons are not for your understanding, but are for My glory.

(176) 5/27/92

Be patient in this gift that I have given you. Let not the evil one have any advantage.

(180-181) 6/7/92

Let the world pass you by. Better to be a servant in

My household than a king in a palace. Call upon My
Holy Mother at every opportunity, for she is the
guide of these times. Listen to her voice as she
speaks to you, for her words are My words. Read of
John the Baptist, for he was the forerunner of My
time. Learn from him of the ways for you. I have
plans for you beyond your understanding. Stay in an
attitude of prayer and be open to My Holy Spirit,
which is the Spirit of Life. Cling to the love of
Christian brothers and sisters, which binds you to
Me.

(183) 6/8/92

Our Lady

Peace you ask for, my son, peace I give you. You
have taken a stand for your Lord and my Lord,
therefore know that we are with you. You come in
humility, you will serve in humility. Keep your eyes
on the Cross, all knowledge comes from the Cross.

(184) 6/20/92

I have taught you much in these last several months.
This is the preparation for what is to come. You have
gone through a period of new conversion. Through
the pain, I have molded you and will make of you a
new forerunner. I will transfer power to you for
direct use against the enemy. Be alert and know that
I will lead you in the glorious moments of My
return.

(187) 6/20/92

Again, I charge you with leadership, but with leadership comes responsibility. This choice has long been
in My plan. You will be led to deeper prayer and
union with Me. At all times you will know that it is
My Spirit at work in you.

(191-192) 7/1/92

Be always obedient, My son, pray, fast, learn, love, and be open to the promptings of My Holy Spirit. Let all things unfold in the natural order.

(193) 7/7/92

My Hand will be seen in all that you do. They will know that it is I who calmed the seas, I who changed the water into wine and I who am the Creator of all things.

(195-196) 7/7/92

Our Lady

My Son speaks from the power of His throne. All who listen will be saved, all who turn a deaf ear will not see the face of the Savior.

Jesus

Call upon My Spirit as you pray. Invoke the intercession of My Holy Mother and all the Angels and Saints and the way of truth will shine forth in all you do and say. Be pleased that I have selected you for this journey. It will not be a smooth and level road, but it will be a path that leads you and others to Me. Be calm, be still and listen to the small, inner voice that speaks to your heart to guide and direct you so that you can be the instrument of My Divine Mercy for many. Forgive those who have hurt you. Love those who are difficult to love, and be Me to everyone.

(212) 7/20/92

I have said that you and I will walk together. Come with Me, step out in faith and I will reveal to you the direction you are to follow. Fear not, I will not lead you astray, for I have called you into service, and for this, you have been chosen. I am the light of the world and I shine down on My people, those who would open their hearts to Me.

(218-219) 8/2/92

You will know of what to do and what to say. My Holy Spirit will fall upon you and My words will be your words. I seek not the wise, but the obedient, the humble and the little ones. I used Peter and Paul to raise the dead, did I not? You are also an apostle, are you not? The only difference between they and you is time!

(221-222) 8/3/92

Let us discourse, you and I. Let us discuss the things that are to come in the days ahead. An anointing will come upon you and you will wear the garments of holiness, transferred to you from My Sacred Heart. You will be consumed with love and compassion for those in need of love and compassion. I have gifted you to carry on My work through My Holy Spirit. Be open to My Spirit and all will go well.

Be a willing vessel from which My power may flow freely into those who do not know Me as their God and Savior, and to increase the faith of the luke-warm. I have chosen you, My son, for your persever-ance and for your faithfulness in visiting Me every day in My Eucharistic form. I need your love and you need My love and together we are united to the love of My Blessed Mother. Go and seek Me this night in total adoration and know that I seek you for My own. Be always at peace!

(231) 8/12/92

Concentrate on prayer and fasting for the needs of

the people. Lay hands on the sick that they may recover as I choose. Follow My desires as I reveal them to you and I will proceed according to My plan. Place the results in My Hands, My "Spiritual Hands", while you place your hands, physically, on My people.

(233) 8/13/92

The "Words of Knowledge" will flow through you, My son, and you will know how to pray.

(293) 9/20/92

Know My little son, that I am working in your life in a powerful way in order for great witness to take place, as well as for the healing of My people. Help all who ask for prayer, even at the inconvenience of your schedule. This is your duty as My servant, and as you extend yourself in this work for Me, I will bless you in many ways.

(295) 9/23/92

This ministry is to be based on the premise that the utmost importance is to be the salvation of souls. All else is secondary to this. My healings and My gifts will be the additional fruits of this ministry.

(308) 9/29/92

My power goes before you to prepare the ones for conversion to My Sacred Heart and the Immaculate Heart of My Mother. You have but to follow through, lay your hands upon them and pray with the heavenly language given to you by Me. I will generate the activity, you will obey and follow Me as I continue to instruct and guide you.

Let all glory become My glory. Peace to you!

(309-310) 9/30/92

You are the Paul and Peter of this day, for I need
and use apostles to correspond with the times.
Humankind changes, I do not change. I heal today
as I healed 2000 years ago. The only difference is
that these times are urgent, as this world is in need
of purging. The sins of today far surpass the sins of
the days when I walked the earth. Hasten to gather
for Me, as many souls as will listen and respond. My
Mother calls them, but most will not hear her.

(311) 10/1/92

Listen to your heart as I speak to you. My people
hurt. Help them. Pray over them. Pray for them.
Bring healing to My flock. It is your mission in this
life. I have brought you out of the desert to free My
people. Be bold! Be Me, for them!

(314) 10/2/92

Our Lady

My little son, do as my Son says. He will prepare the
people who come for prayer and who may be healed,
as is His Will. Ours is a simple task, just "do whatever He tells you". I said these same words to the servants in Cana. Are you not His servant?

Jesus

You are prepared, as My Holy Spirit comes upon
you to anoint your spirit. I will work in you and
through you. What ensues will be My prerogative.
Just be open and do what I expect of you. Love
them, as you pray for them. Be at peace, now!

(317) 10/4/92

I have given you My banner to carry. With it goes My power, which no one can come against. Therefore, from today forward, events will accelerate and you will be part of it all.

(318) 10/5/92

You are among the chosen and I will ask more of you than the others, but I will give you the grace to persevere and the strength to carry out My wishes.

(333) 10/13/92

My son, You are closer to Me, than ever. I will keep you cloaked in holiness as you remain obedient to My Will. You have given your will to Me and I will continue to bless your efforts in the work that I have chosen for you. You will be known for this ministry and all glory will be Mine.

(335) 10/15/92

Stay at peace, My little son, know that your hands will be My hands and that your voice will be My voice, as you pray over My Children. There is no power without My power. It will be Me conducting all, not you.

(337) 10/15/92

Listen to Me, My son, advance rapidly for time grows shorter and shorter. The road is prepared. You have but to step forward and proceed as I direct. I will begin to open doors for you to pass through. Bring My children back to Me. I will give you words, graces and all that you need to fulfill what I desire. You are the standard bearer for My Cross and I will use you in the forefront. Be My warrior of Peace!

(338) 10/16/92

You have prayed well My son. You are learning. Let My Spirit come down upon you this night with emphasis on "new beginnings". You will learn more of the ways of Me. You will understand more of why I am the "God of the Universe". I will nurture you, as you adhere to My words. Be the humble servant I wish you to be.

(360-361) 11/1/92

Our Lady

Pray always and anywhere over my children where the need exists. Lay your hands upon them to heal in the Name of my Son. I will lay my hands upon them, also. Remember always, to invoke the Holy Spirit who guides. We are pleased with your willingness to undertake these works. The gifts will be given to you, my son, doled out as needed.

(366-367) 11/5/92

Our Lady

My little son, all these words will culminate in one unmistakable sign that it is, we, your Jesus and your Mother, who have nurtured and taught you these many months through these many pages and through these many words.

You will know that my Son and I have come to you, both for your edification and to enlist your service in the work of the salvation of souls, through this ministry of prayer for healing, as well as other works. Be pleased that you have been chosen, for it is the Will of my Son to claim whomever He chooses as His servants. You have only to give your "fiat", as I did when Gabriel appeared to me.

(368) 11/6/92

My revelations will be transmitted to you as you extend your hands over My people. All of My love is poured over My people as you pray in My Name and touch them, in My Name. My Mother continues to pray with you.

(370-371) 11/9/92

Through Me, you can move mountains. Does this sound familiar? It is so because "I Am, Who Am", and all things are possible if I deem them to be. Be at ease, be at peace. You are with the "Prince of Peace". My peace is what has kept you in strength and courage. My peace has kept you protected in your spiritual journey.

Let all worries and concerns be borne by Me. I am the healer of all burdens. Pray, fast and I will heal the infirm in spirit, the physically ill and the emotionally crippled that place themselves before Me, through you. Let Me be your rock and your fortress, your rod and your staff and your bread of life.

(374) 11/9/92

Our Lady

The skeptics will be won over and know that it is the works of the Holy Spirit, performed through you. I will lead you to further the ministry. I will be with you in prayer and in protection. Be bold and take charge in the Name of my Son. Let nothing or no one bear down on the truth. My Son continues to bless you and His glory will emerge from this gathering. Peace!

(377) 11/13/92

You will lay your hands upon My people. My Spirit will lead you. My Mother will join you in prayer and the fruits and graces will flow to My people in the areas which will lead them to My Kingdom, the Heavenly Kingdom, to salvation. Again, I say, leave all details in My care and I will choose the path for your ministry.

(378) 11/14/92

Let Our two Hearts protect you against the adversary.

Yours is to obey, Ours is to direct. My son, be persistent. You will persevere. I will see to this. This ministry cannot be destroyed or hindered, as it is of Me and for Me.

My works must continue!

(384) 11/19/92

Continue to be open to the leadings of My Holy Spirit, as the opportunities arise for ministry. Lay hands and pray over My people whenever doors open, for this is to be your life's work. More fruits will come into view and the way will become more clear to you. I will overcome all obstacles that attempt to thwart this ministry. You have but to pray, fast, and look to an increase in faith.

(385) 11/20/92

Listen to Me, My child, My Holy Spirit will descend on My people, as you lay your hands upon them. Your hands will be My hands and the power will flow through you to them.

I will be the determining factor of any results, which are to take place. I minister in Spirit, to My children with love and compassion and I grant you the grace of the same, as you physically impose your hands. My power will come through your voice, as you pray. In essence, you will be an empty vessel, a lowly instrument, pliable clay, to be used at My disposal. This is your service to Me. These gifts are given, always, for furtherance of My glory and for the love I have for My brethren. Touch them, pray over them, leave all else to Me.

(400) 12/8/92

Your spiritual life will increase as you obey, pray and serve Me and My people. This is the manner in which My grace will flow to you. You have tried to follow, with obedience, Me and My Church. For this you will be rewarded and for this. Also, you will be burdened, as are all of My servants. Your joy will be in serving Me, for I AM JOY!

(401) 12/8/92

My son, pray over My people, at all times, whenever the opportunity presents itself, for I have anointed you in this ministry for the conversion of souls that do not know Me and for the deepening of faith for the lukewarm.

(412) 12/20/92

Lean toward understanding the things of the spiritual world, for it is there where you will find My Mother and I, all else matters not. Continue to come to the waters of the spiritual life and you will be blessed abundantly with gifts and favors from on High. My favor rests upon you, My son. Be at peace within Me.

(415-416) 12/23/92

Continue the laying on of your hands upon My people, as this is primarily for the conversion of souls. I will bless them, as I deem it to be beneficial to their eternal lives.

This must continue as I have brought you out of the desert to perform My works, through you. Have I not said "greater things you will do, in My Name"? Always invoke My Holy Spirit and call upon My Mother to pray with you, when you impose your hands upon My people. All that I have instructed you to do must always be done for My glory.

(426) 1/2/93

Let My Spirit come down upon you to anoint you, as you go among My people.

(427) 1/6/93

I will continue to bless the works of the ministry. You will adhere to My Words, in obedience.

(432) 1/9/93

I can do for you even if you cannot do for yourself. Be open to any gifts I wish to give to you. Learn more of Me and My Mother. We are always here for you. We will work through you, in spite of yourself, for the work must be completed. Be always at peace!

(438) 1/23/93

All is being done for My glory and you will continue to be My instrument in preparation for the salvation of others. Live in the light of My peace.

(441) 1/30/93

Our Lady

My son, be holy, as my Son is holy. Know that the only way is through the Sacred Heart of my Son. Be at peace in the knowledge that all will be well as you follow the path, designed particularly for your salvation and service to your God. Look for the signs, look for the gifts, look for us.

(444-446) 2/3/93

You will lay hands on the sick. They will be healed by My power, through you. The conversions will take place. Physical cures will be manifested. My Words never return empty. All will come to pass as events begin to unfold.

Search your heart My little one, do you have the faith to lead of which I have previously spoken? On your shoulders rests the responsibility of many. I have called you among the chosen few.

Will you respond to what I have planned for you or will you go the way of the many others? I have need of you. I have gifted you. I have taught you all these many months, through these many pages and in many other ways. Do not falter, as My Mother and I have designated you to bring about the salvation of many of My people.

Be strong and know that We remain with you through all trials. Turn to Cornelius for assistance. He will be strength to you, along with St. Michael. Be aware of strong signs to be manifested as time continues to wane. You have given your heart to Us. You have given your love to Us. You are trying for this is what binds the three of us together, in love.

Soon change will take place, of which you will be a part.

(455-456) 2/17/93

There, also, is a remnant flock, the faithful who will be enlisted in the army of My Mother, destined to combat and defeat "he of the darkness".

Be a true witness to My Holy Name and compromise nothing as you defend My Commandments. I will open the doors to further ministry as you seek Me in prayer and humility. Let not any pleasures of the world dissuade or seduce you. This world will pass away, but My words will remain.

(460) 2/22/93

All is coming to conclusion. The time of learning is subsiding. My use for you must be completed. The establishment of freedom from your present situation shall be relieved. This new stage will be to catapult you into an area of direct service to Me. For this you must be free to travel, free to be where it is I want you to be.

HE FORGIVES - HE FORGETS

I can't say enough regarding the Sacrament of Reconciliation and Penance. ALL HEALING BEGINS IN THE CONFESSIONAL. I would tell all who come seeking healing to go and reconcile with our God, through the confessing of your sins and telling Our Lord that you are sorry for offending Him.

Some say that they would not want to confess their sins to a priest, because he is merely a human being and that they would instead, confess directly to God. When properly understood, the Sacrament of Reconciliation is recognized as one of God's greatest gifts of love. In the confessional, the priest is the representative of Our Lord and we are truly confessing directly to God. As I am an instrument of healing, through the power of God, so is the priest an instrument of God, to grant absolution for sins, through the power of God. When you leave the confessional and have made a good confession, Jesus not only forgives all of your sins, but also forgets them.

"...all will know me, from the least to the greatest. I will forgive their sins and I will no longer remember their wrongs. I, the Lord, have spoken." (Jeremiah 31:34)

At all of my healing services confessions are heard before mass; and also, after mass when possible.

Jesus' words to Saint Maria Faustina:

"Daughter, when you go to confession, to this fountain of My mercy, the Blood and Water which came forth from My Heart always flows down upon your soul and ennobles it. Every time you go to confession, immerse yourself entirely in My mercy, with great trust, so that I may pour the bounty of My grace upon your soul. When you approach the confessional, know this, that I Myself am waiting there for you. I am only hidden by the priest, but I Myself act in your soul. Here the misery of the soul meets the God of mercy. Tell souls that from this fount of mercy (7) souls draw graces solely with the vessel of trust. If their trust is great, there is no limit to My generosity. The torrents of grace inundate humble souls. The proud remain always in poverty and misery, because My grace turns away from them to humble souls."

(Diary, 1602)

BEFORE HIS EUCHARISTIC PRESENCE

We know that as the Sacrament of Reconciliation is the "beginning of all healing", the Eucharist is the "source of all healing" because Jesus gave His life for us, that we might live and be freed from our sins. Most of the messages I received from Our Lord and Our Lady were given to me while adoring Jesus in His Divine Presence in the Blessed Sacrament.

Pray and listen to the small, still voice speaking to your heart. It is my belief that words from heaven will be given to true believers when they keep company with Jesus, while praying with the heart. I feel most intimate with the Cross during the exposition of the Blessed Sacrament.

There are those, Catholics included, who believe the Eucharist to be symbolic; however, when an ordained priest consecrates the bread and wine, it truly becomes the body and blood of Jesus Christ, Our Lord and Savior.

"For the bread that God gives is he who comes down from heaven and gives life to the world.

"Sir," they asked him, "give us this bread always."

"I am the bread of life," Jesus told them. "He who comes to me will never be hungry; he who believes in me will never be thirsty." (John 6:33,35)

"Jesus said to them, 'I am telling you the truth: if you do not eat the flesh of the Son of Man and drink his blood, you will not have life in yourselves. Whoever eats my flesh and drinks my blood has eternal life, and I will raise him to life on the last day. For my flesh is the real food; my blood is the real drink. Whoever eats my flesh and drinks my blood lives in me, and I live in him. The living Father sent me, and because of him I live also. In the same way whoever eats me will live because of me. This, then, is the bread that came down from heaven; it is not like the bread that your ancestors ate, but then later died. The one who eats this bread will live forever." (John 6: 53-58)

(458) 2/20/93

"As you view Me in My Eucharistic Presence, know that My blessings fall on all those here in attendance. It is for you, and all the world, that I died on the Cross at Calvary.

Meditate on My life and death and you will learn the true meaning of faith. Let all who come to this "little oasis of peace" be blessed, in the Name of the Father, and of the Son and of the Holy Spirit.

(492-494) 4/8/93

If only all My people came to Me as I remain exposed before them. Then they would learn to understand of My love for them and why I suffered for them on the Cross at Calvary. If they meditated and looked into their own hearts, they would know how to enhance their lives to conform with My precepts. None take the time, yet they would spend hours with frivolous pastimes and pleasures. The time will come upon them, and realization will be apparent, that they have missed the hour of My visitation.

Those who view Me in My presence in the Blessed Sacrament will learn of love and compassion and will feel My presence within their hearts. I came upon earth to teach. I died on this earth so that My people may have life.

Most of their choices have gone astray, but the few, the remnant, will remain with Me as did those few who stayed with Me beneath My Cross of suffering. Those who now are helping Me to carry My Cross, through their sufferings, will see eternal life and dwell with Me in the "Eden of Heaven", with the Angels and Saints and the entire Court of Heaven. Live for Me. Look to My Mother for example, and service Me in any area in which I send you to bring conversion to those whom I choose. Be My hands, be

My voice and allow Me to use you in the Divine Plan of the Heavenly Kingdom. The peace I give to you is that which is of My Spirit.

(613) 9/1/93

Our Lady

My Children, I pour my graces down upon you, as you come before my Holy Son in adoration. I am pleased that you give of this time to give reverence to Him who gave all to you. Your lives were replaced with the life of Him, who created the universe. Continue to visit Him in His presence on the altar. Stand in reparation for those whose sacrileges offend His Sacred Heart. You are all my children and I love you. Be at peace!

(743) 5/12/94

You seek My face within the Sacrament of My Eucharistic Presence and yes, there am I. I am here for you and for all the others who remain so faithful to My Sacred Heart and the Immaculate Heart of My Mother. I am here now and will be with you until the end of time.

(784) 8/12/94

If only more would come to visit Me in My Eucharistic Presence. There are so few who are present to adore Me in comparison to the many, many who neglect to even acknowledge My existence. I will bless those who honor and give reverence to Me. The God of all mankind resides in this little housing on this altar, in this Chapel and in all the chapels and places of worship, throughout the world. My heart is hurt, My heart is heavy as so many of My people pass Me by. The remnant will persevere, My faithful will be remembered and will join Me in the "Eternal Kingdom of Love".

I recall the story of one of many Eucharistic miracles; the story entails St. Anthony of Padua, an unbeliever and a mule.

History relates that an unbeliever who rejected the validity of all the Sacraments was one day in a village questioning Saint Anthony regarding the Blessed Sacrament. He vehemently denied the real presence of Jesus Christ in the consecrated Host, while Saint Anthony steadfastly affirmed it. Therefore, both came to agree that, as a test, the choice was to be made by the unbeliever's mule. The mule was not given food for three days and at the end of the fast, a large crowd of believers and unbelievers assembled to witness the outcome.

When the mule was brought before Saint Anthony, the Saint held a consecrated Host before the animal, while the unbeliever tried to feed it hay and oats. The mule paid no attention to the food, but fell to its knees before the Blessed Sacrament. The believers upon seeing this miracle expressed unbridled joy, while the unbelievers present were astounded and confused. It is said that subsequently the unbeliever, along with many other unbelievers, were converted because of the Eucharistic Miracle.

OUR LADY'S PRESENCE

In December of 1992, my dear friend and brother in Christ, Father Bob Rezac, a Consolata Missionary priest, left the U.S.A. to go on assignment to Kenya, East Africa. On his way, he stopped over for a brief pilgrimage in Fatima, Portugal. Father Bob was accompanied by two friends. He then continued onto his mission station in Africa while his companions returned home to the United States. Around Christmas time, his friends called me and said that Father Bob had left a gift for me with them, and that I was to pick it up at their home.

I went to their residence, as directed, and when I opened the package, I found a beautiful 18" statue of Our Lady of Fatima. I promptly showed the statue to a few members of the prayer group where Father Bob formerly served as spiritual director. However, I realized that if I continued to transport the statue from place to place that I would eventually have an accident and perhaps damage part of this beautiful image of Our Lady, as I have been known to be a bit clumsy in handling delicate objects.

I then decided to have two close-up photos of the statue taken, so that it could be viewed by others. When the photographs, taken at approximately the same distance and angle were developed, they appeared to be different from one another. As I examined them more closely, I noticed that Our Lady's head, in the first photo was tilted downward, exhibiting a thin face similar to that of the statue. In the second photo however, her face, which appears fuller and more life-like, is positioned looking straight ahead. Also, the statue has three doves depicted at the feet of Mary; the middle dove somehow maintains different positions in each of the photographs.

I am not claiming that something supernatural took place with regard to these photographs; I am merely stating that the two photographs are at variance with one another. When I asked Our Lady about the pictures, this was her reply:

(457) 2/18/93

Our Lady

The different positions appeared on the photos so that you would know that I am here present with my people, those who are faithful to my Son and follow the messages that flow from my Immaculate Heart. Father Bob is one of my faithful, therefore, I have joined the two of you together within my heart as brothers to my Son, Jesus. Be at peace and relate to my priest son, in the far away land, that my Son and I will be with him in his loneliness as my Son was lonely on Golgotha.

Thank You, Holy Mother!

"THE WEAPON"

As Christians we must have spiritual weapons for our battle against evil.

"For we are not fighting against human beings but against the wicked, spiritual forces in the heavenly world, the rulers, authorities, and cosmic powers of this dark age."

(Ephesians 6:12)

Therefore, the most potent weapon that we possess in our prayer arsenal is the **Rosary**.

Saint Padre Pio, the Capuchin Monk, known and venerated throughout the world, who possessed the stigmata (bodily wounds similar to those of our crucified Lord), and also known by his extraordinary powers of spiritual and physical healings, often called the Rosary, "the weapon".

The Rosary is the "Life of Jesus".
The Rosary is the "Gospel".
The Rosary is the "Good News".

At Medjugorje, Fatima, Lourdes, Garabandal and other apparition sites, Our Lady has encouraged us to pray, daily, the Holy Rosary.

"The disciple whom Jesus loved said to Peter, "It is the Lord!" When Peter heard that it was the Lord, he wrapped his outer garment around him (for he had taken his clothes off) and jumped into the water. The other disciples came to shore in the boat, pulling the net full of fish. They were not very far from land, about a hundred yards away. When they stepped ashore, they

saw a charcoal fire there with fish on it and some bread. Then Jesus said to them, "Bring some of the fish you have just caught." Simon Peter went aboard and dragged the net ashore full of big fish, <u>a hundred and fifty-three</u> in all..."

(John 21: 7-11)

The above number of fish was not 152 or 154 or any other number, but **153**. Could this number mentioned in Holy Scripture be alluding to the Rosary, because the exact number of Hail Mary's in the entire Rosary is **153**.

Coincidence or God incident?

(7-8) 7/24/91

In the course of the next few days, meditate on the mysteries of the Rosary. They will tell you much.

MY HEALING

For many years, my brother who resides across the country in California had to come and visit me. The reason I could not go to visit him was that I had overwhelming fear of flying. However, when his daughter, my niece, set her wedding date, I, with much trepidation, decided to step out in faith and trust in assistance from the Lord. So I went ahead and purchased plane tickets to attend the wedding. A short time later, I went to a healing service in South Buffalo, New York. The building was a large gymnasium with bleachers and Fr. Edward McDonough was the instrument of healing being used by God.

After praying the Rosary, Father asked those in wheelchairs, walkers, etc. to come forward that he may lay hands on them and pray for healing. He used an aspergillum to sprinkle the people as he approached them, prior to the laying on of his hands. Next, he began sprinkling and praying over people who were in the bleacher seats. There were six nuns in upper seats above me, as I was seated in the floor area. As Father prayed over the Sisters, they toppled over one after the other, resembling dominoes in their white and black habits.

He then proceeded downward toward me. I was standing and as he sprinkled me with the blessed water, I became somewhat groggy. When Father reached me, he touched my forehead and I was overcome by the Holy Spirit. I was on the floor, it seemed, for a long time. When I finally arose I had the feeling that I was alone with Jesus, despite the 1,500 or so people present.

After the service, I felt peaceful and serene. While driving home I turned onto a street unfamiliar to me and my headlights caught the name on the street sign "California". Was this my sign from the Lord telling me that my visit to see my brother in California was to be, minus the fear which hindered my air travel for so long? Could it be that I was now free of this bondage?

Well, not only did I fly to California and attended my niece's wedding, but I have since made several trips there as well as flights to Fatima, Portugal; Lourdes, France and St. Sebastian de Garabandal, Spain. I have also made several pilgrimages to Medjugorje in the former Yugoslavia.

I give the glory for my healing to our loving and merciful God.

AN UNEXPECTED GRACE

It was on a late November afternoon in 1997 that I was on my way to a local mall. Quite suddenly, a sense of urgency drew me to want to look at the sun. I had not done this very many times since my last pilgrimage to the village of Medjugorje in the former Yugoslavia.

As I approached the parking lot, I stopped and began observing the sun. I recall that in Medjugorje, I was privileged to see what is known as the "Miracle of the Sun", which refers to a round silver gray, host-like image, that would cover the center of the sun, giving protection from damage to the eyes. Then, various colors from the outer rim would come streaming out of the sun. Following this, the sun would begin to pulsate as the beating of a heart. It would also make various movements known as "dancing in the sky" and then it would seem to descend toward the earth to a point, and then return to its normal position.The phenomenon was first seen at Fatima, Portugal in 1917 when Our Lady appeared to the visionaries, Lucia, Jacinta and Francesco.

I continued to view the sun from that parking lot, and suddenly out of the bottom left of the sun appeared a heart resembling a perfectly shaped valentine. It veered upward and disappeared. A moment later, a second heart burst forth and followed the same path, up and out of sight. Both hearts were of a reddish pink color. I accepted this unexpected experience as a grace from God and would like to think that these hearts were the two "Holy Hearts", Jesus and Mary.

SLAUGHTER OF THE HOLY INNOCENTS

"A sound is heard in Ramah,
the sound of bitter weeping.
Rachel is crying for her children;
she refuses to be comforted,
for they are dead." (Matthew 2:18)

This bible passage refers to the slaughtering of the children in Bethlehem by order of King Herod during the time of the birth of our Lord. His strategy being that the child Jesus, whom he feared as a threat to his reign, would be among those murdered. Some 2000 years later, history is repeated, except that today the innocent unborn are being killed in the wombs of their mothers, by choice, for different reasons.

(202) 7/10/92

The cries of the unborn have saturated the Heavens and the sin cannot be tolerated much longer. Pray for this injustice to end, which is of prime consideration for the action I must take.

(312) 10/2/92

This heinous crime will continue until My intervention, through My Mother, comes about. The evil persists and the evil doers continue to flourish, financially. They will be, however, accountable for their actions as well as those who assist in any way. These atrocities cannot go unpunished. Pray for all involved in this grievous sin against My Sacred Heart.

(517) 5/2/93

My words will be in conjunction with the state of

this world. I cannot allow the destruction of souls through mass sin being committed by those who would murder the unborn.

This crime is beyond all sin, as I am the Creator and I have caused the conceptions of these little ones. Pray for an end to this grievous sin.

(811) 9/26/94

Our Lady

Pray, above all, in love and compassion. Free the prisoners. Heal the afflicted with the disease of cancer. Pray for those who have been victims of abuse — sexual, physical and mental abuse. Pray, too, that they forgive those who have hurt them. Bind the powers of darkness in the Name of Jesus. Pray for the victims of abortion, for the mothers and for those performing abortions. Let the Holy Spirit of my Son permeate this world and infiltrate those places that slaughter the innocent. Heaven calls out for vengeance for this sin of all sins. Pray, pray for an end to this abomination. My Children, pray.

(873) 1/22/95

22nd ANNIVERSARY ROE vs. WADE DECISION

The killing of My innocents will not go unpunished. I came to give life. I will not allow this evil world to continue the slaughter of My "little angels". I WILL allow those who repent of this sin to return to the fold, but for those who ignore My words, better they would have been in the cities of Sodom and Gomorrah than to face Me on the "day of judgment". The cup is spilling over and My mercy is exhausted. Mankind is not responding to My messages, given through My mother; therefore, more

natural calamities will come upon the earth and all will know that My Hand is in the midst of all. Will I find any faith upon the day of My Return?

"Don't you know that your body is the temple of the Holy Spirit, who lives in you and who was given to you by God? You do not belong to yourselves but to God..."
(1 Corinthians 6:19)

"You created every part of me;
you put me together in my mother's womb.
I praise you because you are to be feared;
all you do is strange and wonderful.
I know it with all my heart.
When my bones were being formed,
carefully put together in my mother's womb,
when I was growing there in secret,
you knew that I was there-
you saw me before I was born.
The days allotted to me
had all been recorded in your book,
before any of them ever began." *(Psalms 139: 13-16)*

Let us intensify our prayers for an end to the terrible sin of the killing of innocent babies and that those involved in abortion will repent and reconcile with God. Our Lord, in His infinite mercy and love, will forgive those who are truly repentant. The second part of this action is that when God forgives us, there is an obligation remaining to forgive ourselves.

I have prayed over several women who have acknowledged confessing the sin of abortion; however, they have not reconciled with themselves for this sin. If Our Lord can render forgiveness for this act, then one must forgive oneself, lest we override the gift of His Divine Mercy, the one who died on the Cross for us and forgave us of our sins, Jesus Christ.

THE MYSTERIOUS WAYS OF GOD

When I was in Junior High School, I attended regularly the Perpetual Novena of Our Lady of the Miraculous Medal, at Our Lady of Lebanon Church operated by the Vincentian Fathers of Niagara University, New York. I continued this novena for many years. To this day, I still remember most of the prayers and hymns; however, it wasn't until I recently came upon a little novena booklet that I discovered something rather interesting. I read past the prayers and hymns and found that toward the rear of the booklet a phrase I had not noticed before. The words were "St. Pius X established the Association of the Miraculous Medal".

This to me was a surprising "coincidence," because for more than 10 years I have been conducting monthly healing services in a church named St. Pius X. I use the word "coincidence" with tongue in cheek, as I know that there are no coincidences with God. Moreover, the Vincentian priests of Niagara University have been, among others, celebrating our healing masses for the same 10 plus years. I accept this too, as another "God-incident" in the mysterious ways of Our Lord, Jesus Christ.

ALL UNFOLDS AS PART OF HIS DIVINE PLAN.

(47) 8/24/91

Our Lady

The life of my Son Jesus is the foundation of all Christianity. Those who know of His life and follow His way shall never die but shall have everlasting life.

(148) 4/10/92

More and more people must consecrate their hearts to My Sacred Heart and to the Immaculate Heart of My Mother. Only then can they avoid the coming disasters.

It was raining:

(159) 5/2/92

Listen to the rain, My son. Blessings will fall upon My chosen as rain drops. They have but to follow My ways and discard the ways of the world.

(185-186) 6/20/92

Seek, always, direction from My Holy Mother — the "Queen of Peace". Honor her always. It is she who is liaison between Me and thee. Her appearances are for My Honor and Glory and for the salvation of many souls. Hers is a mission of love and compassion. Be united to her Immaculate Heart which, in turn, is united to My Sacred Heart.

(190-191) 7/1/92

My Holy Spirit will come to those in need of salvation. To gain entrance to Heaven and access to Me, I have loaned My Holy Mother, as messenger and guide, for the most direct route to Me. Those who procrastinate, those with closed hearts, and those who shun Me and My precepts will be lost forever. Therefore, bring as many as will come to the well of living water, so that they may partake of the water of life.

(194) 7/7/92

My Heart is saddened by the loss of many who have not heeded My words and those words given to My Mother by Me for the edification of humanity.

(200-202) 7/10/92

I call upon My people of 'Renewed Faith' to enter into the battleground of spiritual warfare, for the days are coming of which man will choose his direction in eternity. I have sent My Holy Mother to preach the 'Good News' to people, in many parts of the earth. Some listen, many do not. I desire to save My people, but they spurn My love. Therefore, people of faith, pray for those who choose the wealth and power of this world instead of My Kingdom of Holiness.

The day will come when they will believe that I was here, through My Holy Mother, but for most it will be too late. You, who pray in the group of My remnant body, intensify your prayers so that the lost will find their way back to the path leading to My Heavenly Kingdom.

I will lessen the catastrophes foretold, if your prayers and sacrifices reach Me in time.

(204) 7/14/92

The oneness of My Father and the Holy Spirit with Me is further enhanced by the 'Mystical Rose', My

Holy Mother. I ask all of you to join this Circle of Love. You have given of your time, your efforts and your love to come to this place of worship to visit with Me in these most crucial hours, the time of the last days. Those who remain with Me until the end shall be joined to My Court of Heaven in the Eternal Kingdom.

(206-207) 7/16/92

I have chosen the priests of this century who are to be heralds of My "Second Coming". Upon their shoulders rest the responsibility of shepherding My flock into the fold. Those who are obedient will gain My favor, those who fail Me will not see the doors of Heaven. Those of the Royal Priesthood who follow My Mother will be called "Sons", but woe be to the others who lead the faithful away from the truth.

(243-244) 8/2/92

Continue to rebuke the evil one, as he constantly attempts to infiltrate the Church and the faithful. Know that My power and that power which I have given to My Holy Mother will crush the head of the serpent. Nothing will withstand the power which will allow the completion of My Kingdom here on earth. All evil will succumb to the truth as I triumphantly come into My glory in these final hours, in these final days.

(253-254) 8/25/92

The Church will be rent in two. The prophecies of old will come to pass. Leadership will deteriorate. My people will scatter, as of old, as of My time on earth. The little remnant will persevere and keep the faith. All that is to come upon the earth will begin as the people of this world persist in the sins of lust, greed, pride and all other sins against My Commandments.

I have looked the other way at the request of My Mother, but I can no longer ignore the present status of this people of the world. My Sacred Heart is continuously and grievously wounded, time and time again, by those of no faith or those of lukewarm faith. My Mother appears in many places and speaks through many people, but the conversions are not such as to appease My wounded Heart. Pray, pray for eternal life for yourselves and the others, for the days are upon us when there will no longer be choices, as time is fading away. Be at peace with your brothers and sisters. "PRAY FOR PRIESTS".

(402) 12/8/92

Our Lady

If all listen and believe in my Son, that which is about to come upon the earth may and could be lessened. But humankind has no knowledge of what is forthcoming and faith is not increasing. The people have ears tickled with only the things of this world. The evil increases and there is no room in the hearts of men for my Son.

Only purification can change hearts, as is the state of this world. Be vigilante, be at peace, and relate to all to be prepared and to be in the state of grace.

(403) 12/12/92

Be aware of all around you. See the signs of the times. Everywhere there is chaos, everywhere is confusion. Man is hurting his brother in every way imaginable. This world cannot continue against all My commandments, as is happening now. My people must pray, My people must fast, do reparation and convert before it is too late.

(404) 12/13/92

Yes, I am your Lord and your God and I speak to you so that you may transfer My Words to others. It is now a time of deep seriousness, for the days grow short and the work must be escalated. Seek out the lost that they may be garnered into the fold before the "time of mercy" expires.

(406) 12/17/92

I will speak now of more important things, namely the state of this world. Let My people awake, let it be known that they offend Me.

The sands of time are running out and yet no one seems to care. No one seems to listen.

(407) 12/19/92

Do all to bring more to Me, as the time of My Mother comes to conclusion. She returns to Me, soon, from the mission upon which I have designed for her. That which was to be done has not as yet happened. My Children continue in deafness as My messages, through My Mother, ring throughout the world. I cannot help My people, if they do not want to change. Do all for My Honor and Glory.

(408-411) 2/20/92

My son, I come to you as the Spirit of Love. Love is the greatest force in the world. It was My Love that redeemed the whole of humanity for those who chose to accept Me. I died to bring life to all, but only those who truly believe understand this sacred mystery. I have strong words for you My son: you are to do My Will in departing to where I will send you to minister to My people, My poor souls who are to be led to the path of conversion. I am choosing you for this mission. Your hands will be My Hands, your voice will be My Voice, your mind and heart will be under the guidance of My Holy Spirit. My power will come upon you and through you to rest upon they who need My grace and peace, those who will be transformed into what I want them to be.

My Kingdom thirsts for the unsaved, before the terrible times arrive and the "period of grace" will no longer be. This accomplishment must be done by the remnant flocks that exist throughout the various parishes who believe that "My Second Coming" is eminent and close at hand. My people seek the pleasures of this earth, but soon all will pass away and only the light of My Spirit will illuminate the universe.

For those who believe, little is to be feared. For those who do not believe, let them know that My wrath will come upon them for they choose other gods over Me. This I will not tolerate and I claim Myself as their God.

Let My people go to My Holy Mother and believe in the messages I have sent through Her, as these are My Words given to the Queen of Peace for the salvation of mankind. Soon more signs will come upon the earth, telling of events to come. Some will adhere to My ways; however, the majority who are in the material world will deny Me again. They will be lost. They will be as the chaff burned in the fire.

Pray for them! Pray for them! Pray for them!

(414) 12/23/92

Our Lady

I will come as the "Queen of Heaven". I will be bathed in light. There will be angels about. I will bring messages for the sake of salvation.

I will bind my remnant flock together. The stout-hearted will remain, the faint-hearted will depart, but has it not always been so?

(416) 12/23/92

Pray over them and <u>reveal the messages</u> as there will be a remaining remnant people there as there will be remnants everywhere. This plan constitutes the army of My Mother who will crush the head of the serpent, as She is victorious in the final battle. Pray much, fast much, offer all to Me, and assist to prepare others for the time of My glorious return.

(417) 12/23/92

Anything other than peace is not of Me, My son; therefore, put all confusion aside as the evil one attempts to dissuade you from My leadings. When the peace comes, know that My presence and the presence of My Mother will permeate your very being. There will be signs, indelible signs of which no one can deny. It is through these signs that the authenticity will prevail.

I love you!
My Mother loves you!
Our peace goes with you!

(418) 12/26/92

Let not trepidation take over, but be still and listen to all that We speak of in order to complete all of the plan of salvation.

(419) 12/27/92

As these hours go by, as you remain here and pray, know that all the prayers of the faithful are instrumental in the gathering of souls into My Heavenly

Kingdom. It is a heavenly sound to listen to all of you praying in worship to Me.

(420-423) 12/31/92

Are you at a loss now, My son? Know that we are still with you, My Mother and I. Through you, sinful as you are, we will send words for the edification of the remnant flocks. The time of "great mercy" comes to conclusion at a rapid pace. There seems to be no repentance and no conversion to My Sacred Heart, only few have decided to follow Me. There will be wailing in the streets, they will seek Me, but it will be too late for many. I will give a great grace here at this place of worship. She will be with you and they will know. This will not be a mistaken sign as it is My wish to confirm all that has been written.

Be at peace, for I have chosen you to lead in the conversion of many. My priest son knows that this is so and will act accordingly. All this is part of My Divine Plan, for the remaining faithful of these times.

Our Lady

My Son directs you as He unfolds the events to be used in the salvation of the distant souls. I, the Mother of God and your heavenly Mother, will watch over you and pray with you, as you minister to my Son's people, who are my children also. Be not anxious in anything of your earthly life as I will direct all for the good of my children.

The heavenly messages will be relayed to the flocks shortly. It will be for the uplifting of their spirits, for those who believe. It is of no consequence for the unbelievers, as their faith level would not allow the messages to penetrate their hearts; therefore, continue to seek us, continue to pray, continue to fast and continue to seek a level of higher faith and let your

Heavenly Father and your heavenly Mother lead you as you pursue this path of the Spirit of Holiness. There will be more healings, more conversions, and more graces emerging from the ministry given to you by my Son, Jesus. Always, and first, comes the Glory of my Son, followed by the conversion of His people in their spirits, minds and bodies. All is done according to the Divine Will of my Son, who brings all good to those who persevere in His Holy Name.

(424-425) 12/31/92

The last days of this year will be followed by the apostasy in the true Church as known to you and the faithful. The beginning of the final days commences as the world grows deeper into sin. The people set their faces as flint against one another. Love becomes almost non-existent, except for the few immersed in My love and the love of My Mother. Thoughts of eternal life are foreign to most. My Mother continues to attempt to show the misdirected to the path of My glory. Some of the captives will be set free, but the spiritually blind will remain bound to this world. Let all the faithful be engaged in the work of assisting My Mother in the task of the salvation of souls, as this New Year begins. This will come about by continual prayer, fasting and penance. Help bring to me as many as may be saved.

(429-430) 1/6/93

Our Lady

I speak to you, my son, with a mother's heart. A heart full of compassion for those who do not know of the love of my Son. Please, continuously strive to bring them into the realm of my Son, Jesus. If they only knew what bliss awaits them in the union with Our God, they would put all aside and return to the fold. We must pray fervently, you and I, when you impose your hands, so that satan will not snatch them into eternal damnation. Words will be given to you to enhance the power of this ministry. Follow the Holy Spirit as He leads you to those whom my Son will call into the Kingdom. My thoughts are the same, as my Son's thoughts, as we are one in all things. Be always at peace in the Sacred Heart and in the Immaculate Heart.

(433) 1/10/93

My Spirit will be the only spirit in the "New Era of the Terrestrial Paradise." Let all My people come to Us and know that they will be protected with My Precious Blood and be under the Mantle of My Holy Mother. Lead lives of holiness and know that I am God.

(436) 1/17/93

We have to speak more often, Come to Me in adoration and in awe as is what is expected for the God of the Universe. We will speak of all that concerns My people for their good, which is conversion, which, in turn, is salvation of their souls. I will direct you further as we speak.

Go in peace!

(437) 1/21/93

You come to me tonight, do you My son? We have not spoken as of late. Have you forgotten Me? Let us again begin a love tryst; you, Me, and My Mother. I come to you as the King of kings. It is through Me that this world will be purified for the evil that has pervaded this earth. It has gone far beyond what I am able to endure. Let My people come to Me as the hour grows late. Only repentance, conversion and total abandonment to Me will lessen what is to come.

(439) 1/24/93

There are danger signals ahead. Proceed with caution. He of the nether world attempts to dissuade you from the ministry, prepared by Me to bring salvation to My people. Persevere, My son, look not to the left nor to the right, but keep your eyes on Me. I am your foundation, your protection and your strength. Together we will withstand the fiery darts of the evil one. Be at peace in knowing that My Mother and I look after you.

(440) 1/28/93

My words are few as now is a time for prayer and meditation. Let Me speak only on what is to come, sooner than is expected. It is the purification of those who will not listen and will not bow to My words.

Let them who have ears, hear.

(448) 2/6/93

I pass these words to you, My son. Let it be known that My wishes for renewed dedication to My Holy Presence upon the altar commence as it is imperative in these times. Seek assistance from others; however, it must begin for continuance of the salvation of souls. You will be soon viewing more evidence of Heavenly Presence as We reign among you.

(449) 2/7/93

It is time for listening. Time for all to heed the call of My Mother. Her messages fall on deaf ears, except for the few remaining, the remnant.

Seek, My son, to bring others to Me through My Holy Mother, by whatever means are at your disposal. Collaborate with My priest son and, together, there will be a gathering of My lost sheep. Go in peace!

(450) 2/13/93

Can you come to Me in silence any more? I miss you. <u>All I say to you will be related one day</u>. Listen carefully as I tell you of great events to take place before the hour of chastisement arrives. There will be signs in all of the churches. There will be signs in the hearts of the faithful. There will be signs to confirm that My Mother has been in the world, among you, to bring My messages to those who would listen.

(451-452) 2/14/93

See the birds flocking to obtain food. This is what My people should be doing, following their example, flocking to Me for food, the "Bread of Life", so that they may be prepared for the coming days. Feed them, My son, in cooperation with My priest son. Feed them with My healing power, which leads to conversion to Me. Feed them with My words. Feed them with My Sacrament of sincere confession. Most of all, feed them with My presence exposed on the altar. Let them know that I await them, to take souls to My Bosom, through the Immaculate Heart of My Mother. Plant seeds of love within their hearts, whenever the occasion permits. Work diligently, as time is quickly passing and many need to be brought to salvation.

Assist all who seem lost and are looking for spiritual aid. Plan events with My priest son, as he is among the few of My priests sons who will lead the remnant flocks. Be united in Christian love to those who would seem to be willing to promote My Sacred

Name to the masses. In these final days, let My Messages reign supreme in the hearts of the faithful, for these few will gain heavenly favor in My Kingdom. Go in peace, in the Name of the Father and of the Son and of the Holy Spirit.

(453) 2/14/93

Our Lady

My son, I tell you now of the souls I seek to bring to my Son. They are those who have gone the way of the world, the way of seeking bodily pleasures, and the way of seeking material satisfaction. Seek them out and lead them to my Son.

(482) 3/24/93

Our Lady

Listen to my Son for His words are not idle words. He is seeking to garner those who have not yet heard His words, those who still remain hard-hearted and those whose pride has not been broken.

(487-488) 3/30/93

Our Lady

He is offended more and more, each day. Men find more and new ways to pierce His Heart, while passing Him by in their materialistic world of pride and greed. Many events will take place and shake this universe from its complacent foundations. Remain in a state of grace. Tell the flock to remain in a state of grace. Help to convert any of my priest sons, when the occasion arises. I wish to lose not one of them.

(509) 4/23/93

Be still and listen to My voice. It is through My
Sacred Heart that peace will return to this world.
There is no other way that man can devise that
would return peace upon this earth. Only through
purification may all be rendered sinless, by what is
prophesied in My Word, "My Second Coming". My
words of warning are not heard, My Mother's messages are not put into practice and this era of sin
continues at an escalating pace. My little ones, pray
for the lost sheep so that during the final hours, they
will repent and return to the fold.

(625) 9/16/93

I come to you as the "King of Peace". All remains
serene if I deem it so; however, the time of mercy is
drawing to a close and My children have not made
many correct choices. Most choose the world rather
than My Cross. I will not force My Will upon them.
They must give of their free will to Me.

(632) 9/30/93

Tonight we will begin to see new events take place.
Some for the good of the flock, some to the dismay of
the world. Let those who have not yet found Me
begin to seek Me, for the end is closer at hand than
some would like to believe. The beginnings of the
end will shake many, but hearts will still remain
hard.

(642) 10/12/93

Rest yourself, My son, before Me in My
Eucharistic Presence and let Me permeate your
very being. Allow Me to be all that you need for
survival in this world. You cannot fathom what is to

befall this corrupt universe. This is not what I created in the beginning.

(653) 11/4/93

This is the time of listening, but does anyone listen? My Mother has come to you for over 12 years in the little village between the mountains, but her words seem to be in vain. A dark cloud will cover this whole earth unless men turn to Me. This message is urgent as I intend it to be so.

(672) 12/21/93

The faithful, they are to be My people of these last days, the staunch prayer warriors on the side of holiness. They will form together the flock of believers for the final days. Come to Me, My little ones, and learn more of Me, then go out and extend the Good News to others.

(675-676) 12/26/93

No one can know what is in store for this perverse world. It has gone beyond all limits as to the disobeying of My Commandments. There is little left for humanity to accomplish against My precepts. There will come a time in which most will wish they had changed their lives during the time of My Great Mercy, but the lateness of the hour will prevent them from doing so. They will have lost the time of love for Me.

(690) 2/2/94

Will you listen when I say this world, as you know it, will not be the same. What is coming will change the face of this earth. All will be engulfed in chaos and tragedy. Only those faithful to the messages of My Mother will merit the protection of My Kingdom. Be prepared, lest you be among the lost souls who have deafened their ears to My Words.

(702) 2/19/94

Our Lady

Allude to all that I have taught you in the past. I have called you out of darkness, into the light of service for the Kingdom. In these times of prophesied trials and sufferings, those of the remnant will be called into service more and more. This small army of mine will break forth in power and might and will be the demise of the enemy in these, the last days. I come as the Mother of all people, although most do not acknowledge me as such. For those who choose for conversion, there will be protection and peace. Woe be to all who choose this world and its materialism over the Kingdom of eternal life with my Son.

(704) 3/1/94

Come to Me all who are weary and in thirst, and I will quench your thirst with My Living Waters. Be bound to one another, My remnant people, for the time is near at hand, the time of which I have spoken.

(709) 3/10/94

And so we begin anew, My speaking, your listening. Much more is to be done for the Kingdom. Free yourselves, My Children, from the ties of the world so that you may be about My Father's business leading souls to eternal life in Me. This is the final hour, recognize it and be glad.

(713) 3/15/94

Our Lady

The pleas of my Son do not reach many hearts. For this, there will be no mercy, except the mercy of fear. Seek those on the path to perdition and endeavor to bring salvation to them.

(727) 4/8/94

Our Lady

Have no concern regarding earthly problems for my Mantle will overshadow all. Be concerned only for spiritual values, for it is these that will lead you to eternal holiness. The blood and water which gushes forth from my Son will cleanse all that needs to be cleansed for those who seek conversion and salvation.

(745) 5/16/94

Our Lady

My son wishes that all who persevere in prayer renew their efforts to bring more souls to the flock so that my cohort will increase, as the days of battle are in sight. St. Michael will prepare, as will all the Saints in Heaven, for the time of decision nears and the lines will be drawn.

(749) 5/31/94

Our Lady

As you come to pray, my child, I ask that you re-double your efforts in the cause of lost souls. The time grows shorter each day. The justice of my Son will come to pass sooner than most anticipate. Mercy has been extended beyond limit.

(753) 6/7/94

Our Lady

Yes, today I say to you and the others, fortify your-selves for the times are coming when my Son's justice will prevail. Woe to those who do not heed the signs.

(754) 6/11/94

I yearn to see the results of the prayers and sacrifices of My faithful. Never before were prayers needed as they are now, at this time. The only sure way of salvation, for the lost, is prayer. Look to My Mother to lead you to prayer and to Me.

(766) 7/9/94

The wars will increase as the state of humanity decreases in compassion. More calamities will unfold as were prophesied and in conformity with My Word.

(769) 7/17/94

Our Lady

These are the days in which all must turn to my Son, for it is the final time for conversion. Receive the King of kings now, as His mercy was extended for those not understanding His love for them. But the cup has overflowed and the time of His justice is upon us. Tarry no more, but come to Him who holds the key to eternal life.

(789) 8/20/94

Our Lady

My peace is available to those who will listen to the

message of my Son, Jesus. Those who shun the message will have to accept the consequences. Time and again, I have come to spread words of salvation, but many have ears open only to the world.

(806) 9/18/94

Clearly the future will be the times of suffering, conversion, followed by an era of peace. I call the people of these times to prayer to stave off these sufferings or to at least lessen what is to come. Convert to My Sacred Heart through the Immaculate Heart of My Mother.

(820-821) 10/10/94

I deem you worthy to be a son of the Most High. Your consistency is needed to fulfill all that the future holds for you. Be still and know that I am God, that I am present before you in body and blood as I was when I walked this earth. You and My beloved others are commissioned to spread My Gospel to the ends of the earth. This commission was given to My first apostles, 2000 years ago. Every age produces apostles, but I remain the same. You will be among the last of My apostles for these are the days of finality. Prepare for the New Pentecost for My coming is imminent. My Mother pleads for sinners and My Vicar of these times travels at risk to gather souls to conversion, but ears are deaf and eyes are blind to the Good News of salvation. This planet will be shaken to its core, then many ears will hear and many eyes will see. Yet, the hearts of still many will remain unchanged. Woe to those stiff necked, when My judgment is meted out. There will be wailing in the streets, as the era of My mercy is replaced by the era of My justice. Pray for the innocents, pray for their mothers, pray for the murderers of My unborn. Look to Me for all answers, large and small. Pray, fast and sacrifice and I will gift you for the coming events of these times. Relate these words to those whom I have united to you. Peace to you, My children.

THE YOUNG PRIEST

I have not known Father Art Mattulke as long as I have known other priests; however, I feel a close bond between us for various reasons. He is the youngest among my priest friends, but I feel that I can draw on his mature wisdom. In discussions with Father Art, I realize that we are on the same page in our views regarding the Church, the Holy Father, Our Lady, the Blessed Sacrament, confessions and healing. A story involving Father Art, in the March 2000 issue in our Diocesan paper, *The Western New York Catholic*, (article written by Patrick J. Buechi and Mark Ciemcioch, WNYC staff reporters) seems worthy of being repeated as it attests to the character of this young priest:

PRIEST ATTACK ON DAY OF LOVE

Mysterious man attacks Father Arthur Mattulke at St. Margaret Parish

Father Arthur J Mattulke, parochial vicar of St. Margaret parish in Buffalo, is recovering from his attack on the morning of St. Valentine's Day. While preparing for morning Mass, Father Mattulke, 30, was allegedly attacked by a 27 year-old North Buffalo man. Father Mattulke was beaten with a processional cross, then stabbed in the back with an aspergillum, or holy water sprinkler, between 6:30 and 7:00 a.m. Bishop Henry J. Mansell praised Father Mattulke for "defending the tabernacle, defending the altar, defending the sanctuary." The bishop went on to say, "We have a hero, a priest hero." Although Father Mattulke required no surgery, he went away with several stitches. He stayed at the hospital overnight for observation and is expected to make a full recovery.

Father Mattulke was struck in the head seven or more times with the processional crucifix and was stabbed in the lower left back with the aspergillum. The man chased Father Mattulke into a bathroom, where he allegedly kicked down the locked door and attacked him again. Buffalo police officers Obed Casillas and Anthony Figueroa were on the scene within minutes of the attack being reported by Ann Fusco, who was at the church during the incident. Upon entering St. Margaret's, the officers encountered Father Mattulke running from the rectory. Father Mattulke told police he was a priest, but the assailant followed and also said he was a priest. After a moment of confusion, the officers determined that the perpetrator's statements were false and arrested him. The man was charged with first-degree assault, third-degree criminal trespass, and fourth-degree criminal possession of a weapon. According to Buffalo Police Public Information Officer Lt. Larry Baehre, no motive has been determined thus far. "With a person of this mind set, I don't know what the motive was, and I think the only way to determine that is with a competent psychiatric examination," he said. Bishop Mansell praised the work of the Buffalo Police and staff at Erie County Medical Center for their quick action and thorough work. Father Mattulke, the son of Gail and the late Roger Mattulke, attended SS. Peter and Paul Parish in Williamsville. It was there that he first began teaching religion classes. While attending Erie Community College North Campus, Father Robert Yetter suggested that Father Mattulke consider the priesthood. Father Mattulke then moved, at Father Yetter's suggestion, to Pope John Paul II Residence in Buffalo while he attended Canisius College, Buffalo. After graduating, Father Mattulke entered Christ the King Seminary in East Aurora. He spent his summers serving as parochial vicar at St. Gabriel Parish in Elma. His field education included serving at Collins Correctional Facility in Helmuth, and at Millard Fillmore Hospital as chaplain intern. In May of 1997, Father Mattulke was ordained a priest by Bishop Henry Mansell. Father Mattulke continued to serve at St. Gabriel's. He continued his involvement with the Catholic youth by being active in the parish education program and youth group. In July 1998, Father Mattulke was assigned to serve St. Margaret Parish as parochial vicar. Father Mattulke is also a fourth degree member of the Knights of Columbus. Prior to his passing, Father Mattulke's father Roger once said of him, "He always had a real love for his fellow man." Bishop Mansell expressed his concern for the troubled man's future. "We pray for (Father Mattulke's) attacker," he said. "We don't know what his mental state is. This is a reminder that these things happen from time to time. How do you prevent somebody from walking in for morning Mass?"

Father Mattulke praises those helping him in time of need in statement

I would like to express my deepest gratitude and praise to Our Lord for watching over me and for being so close to me through this terrible ordeal.

I have become so aware of God's presence in my life through the struggle. I felt a complete sense of peace as I truly thought that I would lose my life that morning. This sense of peace allowed me to keep a clear enough head to keep him running after me and away from others.

I have heard that some have referred to me as a hero. I agree that through this situation many heroes have arisen. I am quite aware that Miss Ann Fusco, who so quickly called the police, is certainly a hero. Bishop Henry J. Mansell and Msgr. James Kelly, who were so present to me and my family during this ordeal, are certainly heroes in God's service. The police who responded so quickly to the scene are all heroes. If they had been seconds later, I know that I would not be here to say "thank you." The ambulance crew, the doctors, nurses, aides, the entire staff at ECMC hospital all are heroes for the ways that they shared their love with me. The many people who have not ceased in offering thoughts and prayers for my recovery are all the quiet heroes that make up the strength and backbone of God's people.

To all the heroes in my life, I would like to say "thank you" from the bottom of my heart. It is because of your heroic actions that I still have my life and that I may continue to praise God as His priest. Many school children have written such beautiful words and thoughts in cards that they have sent to me. A few of these asked if I still loved the man who did this, and do I want God to punish him for this. I love all God's people and "yes," this does apply to the young man. I have not stopped remembering him in my prayers and asking that God be with him as his struggle begins. I am sure that he is a deeply troubled young man who so needs all of our prayers. And so, as I continue to heal and recover, I ask that we turn our prayers for this man that God may be with him and that he may seek the Lord's love and forgiveness.

In conclusion, my family and I are completely overwhelmed by the generous outpouring of love, prayer, support and gifts that we have received. They have brought such an immense sense of peace and warmth of love that has allowed me to relax and heal. I truly thank you all and appreciate your love.

Father Art Mattulke

It is ironic that this incident took place on St. Valentine's Day and that I was to conduct a healing service at this church that very night. Needless to say, that the healing mass was canceled because of this tragic situation. Incidentally, my ministry has held previous healing services at St. Margaret's Church, where there have been some reported healings.

Father Art Mattulke is an example of the caliber of new young priests ordained in the diocese and I pray that more vocations to the priesthood will emerge to continue in the works of service to our Lord, Jesus Christ.

A LESSON IN HUMILITY

(864) 1/6/95

(Question) The choice is yours. Only good comes to My faithful who extend themselves to see Me in "Holy Pilgrimage". If it is in your power to visit the places where I have sent My Mother with My messages of love and salvation, then let it be done. If this is not to be, My "Holy Intervention" will take place.

(892) 2/26/95

You shall deliver unto My people across the sea, a message of healing and consolation. It will be within the realm of what I am accomplishing in these last days. You will encounter several events which will take you and the others, closer to My Sacred Heart and to the Immaculate Heart of My Mother. Be at Peace!

The above messages were received prior to a 1995 Easter week pilgrimage that would take my friends and I to three Marian sites in Europe: Fatima, Portugal, Lourdes, France, and San Sebastian de Garabandal, Spain. This tour was probably one of the largest, as it consisted of approximately 500 pilgrims and 12 priests. Each of the holy places presented various spiritual experiences. We arrived in Lisbon, Portugal and were greeted by our tour guide and were first taken to the birth place church of St. Anthony of Padua. Next we went on to inspect the magnificent Monastery of St. Jeronimo and the unique Belem Tower. We then went on to the church of St. Stephen at Santarem, for Holy Mass, which is called the "Church of the Holy Miracle", because of what occurred regarding a "Bleeding Host":

The story of the "Bleeding Host" takes place in the 13th century where there lived in the village of Santarem a poor woman unhappy and miserable because of her unfaithful husband.

136

Frustrated and weary of so much unhappiness that she decided to consult a sorceress for aid. The sorceress promised the woman that all her difficulties would end if she would bring to her a consecrated Host. The woman agreed to this sacrilegious exchange and after going to church and receiving communion, she removed the Host from her mouth and carefully wrapped it in her veil and left the church.

On the way to where she was to meet the sorceress, the woman was unaware of the great drops of blood that fell from her veil. Several bystanders, who saw the Blood inquired why she was bleeding so profusely and offered to assist her. The woman avoided them and rushed home in a confused state and upon arriving there hid the bloody veil and its contents in a wooden chest.

However, in the middle of the night she and her husband awoke and saw the house lit up by mysterious rays emanating from the wooden chest. Upon seeing this strange sight the woman confessed her sin to her husband and they both spent the remaining hours of the night, upon their knees, in adoration.

At daybreak the parish priest was informed and people from near and far rushed to the woman's house to view this miraculous event. The Host was then taken, in procession, to the Church of St. Stephen where it was placed in a small case of wax.

Some time later, when the Tabernacle was opened for adoration of the Blessed Sacrament, another miracle had taken place. The wax case was found broken in pieces and the Holy Sacrament was found enclosed in a crystal pyx. The pyx was placed in a gold-plated silver monstrance for its preservation and is displayed for the veneration of pilgrims.

The Church of St. Stephen is now named "The Church of the Holy Miracle".

It was an awesome experience for us to be in the presence of the Venerated Relic of the "Bleeding Host". There were many tears, as we pilgrims were privileged to kiss the monstrance that housed the miraculous Host. One woman was overcome to the point of resting in God's Holy Spirit as she came into contact with the relic.

We continued on our journey to Fatima and celebrated

Holy Mass in the little Chapel of Apparitions at the Cova da Iria. It was at this site that Our Lady first appeared to the three children – Lucia, Jacinta, and Francesco. We then visited the Basilica to visit the tombs of St. Francesco and St. Jacinta. Sister Lucia, the only living visionary, resides in Coimbra, near Fatima, as a cloistered nun. Next, we continued on to San Sebastian de Garabandal, a small hamlet of some 80 or so humble dwellings located in the Cantabrian Mountains of northwest Spain.

"On June 18, 1961, four girls, Mari Loli Mazon (12), Jacinta Gonzalez (12), Mari Cruz Gonzalez (11) and Conchita Gonzalez (12) were playing on the edge of the village when they heard a sound like thunder. Suddenly, there appeared before them a dazzling angel. He said nothing and quickly disappeared. Visibly shaken, the girls ran to the village church and the apparition soon became known. Over the next twelve days, the angel appeared to them several more times and then on July 1, he spoke for the first time, announcing that on the following day, the Blessed Virgin would appear to them as "Our Lady of Mount Carmel".

News spread quickly. On July 2, many priests were among the numerous visitors who joined the villagers to witness the great event. At about 6:00 p m., the children were headed for the place where they had been seeing the angel when the Blessed Virgin appeared with an angel on each side. They recognized one of the angels as the one who had been appearing to them (later identified as St. Michael the Archangel), and the other looked identical. They spoke openly and familiarly with their Heavenly Mother and prayed the Rosary in her presence. Over the next year and a half she would appear hundreds of times, frequently appearing several times in a single day. It is here in San Sebastian de Garabandal (at the nine pines), that a special "miracle" will reportedly take place. After the "miracle", a permanent visible supernatural "sign" will remain at the pines, until the end of time.

After spending two days in San Sebastian de Garabandal, we left for the last leg of our journey to Lourdes, France. St. Bernadette was born in 1858 in the small town of France called Lourdes. As a meek innocent child, she was privileged to see the Virgin Mary in a grotto eighteen times and to be instructed by her with many heavenly messages. As a religious at the Convent of Nevens, she offered herself as a victim

138

for the conversion of sinners. Our Lady came to Bernadette as the "Immaculate Conception", affirming the truth of the dogma recently proclaimed by the Church.

Since then, millions of pilgrims from all over the world have traveled there yearly to take part in the candlelight procession at this shrine whose waters have been known for healing. We visited the chapel of St. Bernadette, the Basilica of St. Pius X, and had the opportunity to bathe in the healing waters of Lourdes. The uphill climb while in prayer during the Stations of the Cross was exhilarating as we viewed the life-like figures of Our Lord and the participants of that time. The in-depth accounts of the Apparitions of the Blessed Virgin Mary in Fatima, Lourdes and Garabandal may be found in several books and videos by various authors. I thank Our Lord and Our Lady for bringing me to these holy places and also for allowing me the opportunity to lay on hands and pray over His people while on pilgrimage.

Messages received while on pilgrimage:

(910-912) Fatima, Portugal

Palm Sunday 4/9/95

As you seek Me in these holy places of which My Mother appeared to bring My messages, I will enhance your prayer life and the ministry of love and compassion that I have commissioned you to fulfill in your life of service to Me. You will be transformed into new life in My Holy Spirit. This life will come also at the behest of My Mother, whom you revere and love with your heart. I will infuse new life in the ministry, as you carry on these works which I began when I walked the earth. All of you, My little ones, will be partakers of my restorial work. You will be directed by My Spirit as you remain on this foreign soil and as you return to your native land. All of you will conduct yourselves in a manner befitting witness to My Holy Name. Much attention must be given to My lost ones, and through your efforts, many will return to Me. I am the God of Salvation

139

and it is truly, I, you receive in the form of bread and wine. Yes, you partake of My Body and Blood through the hands of My priest sons, of whom I love so much. And yes, I will even heal those priest sons who have offended Me, if they would but come to My Confessional and repent of all which offends Me, for they, too, are only of human form.

They are not only special to Me because I have created them, but also because they are of the line of My Royal Priesthood. Pray for them, My children. I bless you in the Name of the Father and of the Son and of the Holy Spirit, and know that My Mother, the Mother of all mankind, loves you and is happy you came to visit in these, the places of ever spreading devotion to My Sacred Heart.

(914) Reinosa, Spain

Good Friday 4/14/95

Learn more of Me, My son, for it is not because you traveled so far, but because you came seeking Me. Let My Mother guide you through further instruction, as she reflects My wishes to you. Seek out the "little one" again and pray for him in physical contact, for you will be the instrument I will use for his betterment, but know, also, that his witness contains My power, as I heal in many ways. You will be empowered further as you leave these lands.

Our Lady

You will know me better as we pray, each time, for others, did you not know this?

The Lord speaks of the "little one" in the above message. This brings me to the title of this chapter, the story of which remains all so clearly in my memory.

It was in Fatima, in the Cova da Iria, that I first met little Mark, one of 500 pilgrims in our tour. He was a boy approximately eight to ten years of age, confined to a wheel chair, because of a debilitating disease. Mark's mother and father accompanied him everywhere and it was apparent that to them, he was not a burden but a blessing. Someone had mentioned to Mark's parents that I was in the healing ministry and so they asked if I would lay on hands and pray over their son. But before I began, his mother said,"You know, sometimes Mark prays over people", and at that, I knelt before him and asked him to pray over me. He laid his trembling hand on my head, and with a stuttering voice, prayed over me. This act brought tears to my eyes and I experienced the most humbling moment of my life. After this, I prayed over Mark not only there in Fatima, but also in Garabandal and in Lourdes, as Jesus arranged for our paths to cross.

I think of Mark, often, as a little angel, sent from God to teach me humility of heart. I don't know if the Lord has healed Mark, but what I do know is that Mark, through his infirmity, touched many hearts on that pilgrimage. It seems that whenever I speak of little Mark, tears well up in my eyes, as I recall the words of Jesus, "And a little child shall lead them."

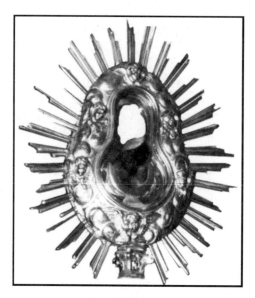

Bleeding Host
in the Church of the Holy Miracle,
Santarem, Portugal

Cova da Ira - Fatima, Portugal

The Nine Pines - San Sebastian de Garabandal, Spain

Praying over "Little Mark".
San Sebastian de Garabandal, Spain

Grotto of Our Lady of Lourdes - Lourdes, France
("The Immaculate Conception")

WOMEN OF PRAYER

God completed forming this ministry of healing by enlisting others in this cause. These would consist of Charlene, Angie, Joanne, Maria, Mary, Dominique and Marianne. All reside in the Diocese of Buffalo, New York. Charlene is from Amherst, Angie from Williamsville, Joanne from Grand Island, Maria from Hamburg, Mary is from Getzville, Dominique from Depew and Marianne is from Williamsville. The Lord fit them into my life according to His Divine Plan.

They perform all the tasks that are needed to operate this ministry, but most of all, they are women of deep faith and possess the various charisms of the Holy Spirit. I am privileged to have these women of prayer support me in the works of love and compassion for the glory of God.

(55-56) 9/1/91

Love is akin to compassion, this is what is needed for the ministry I have prepared for you. Others will help you and be involved.

(65) 9/8/91

I am placing people in your life to sustain you. They will be part of your permanent life. I will guide you and them.

(134) 2/28/92

The pieces will fit into place as you pray together. Words of knowledge will flow and the ministry will begin. Follow what I have taught you. You have absorbed well.

(143) 3/22/92

I will bless you and the ministry as you go forward
to do battle for Me.

(181) 6/7/92

Call upon My Holy Mother at every opportunity, for
she is the guide of these times. Listen to her voice, as
she speaks to you, for her words are My words.

(298) 9/25/92

My choices are not made frivolously and I choose
those of whom I can rely upon, those already prepared by Me.

Also, my ministry is fortunate to have an intercessory
prayer group, comprised of young, married persons, who support us in prayer, as we minister in the churches, or anywhere,
where prayer and the laying on of hands is needed.

(481) 3/24/93

Others will share in this ministry. They will be intercessory warriors of prayer as you lay your hands
and pray in My Name.

(499) 4/11/93

Seek help in My requests, as there are those who are
dedicated, in love and compassion, to My Holy
Name. These will be the intercessory prayer warriors
which I have spoken of late.

(526) 5/12/93

Our Lady

Know also, that we will be with you as you minister to those who have need of prayer and conversion. We will bless you and all who work in this ministry, as this was founded by my Son, Jesus, for the salvation of souls.

(527-528) 5/13/93

These are precisely the little ones I have put in your path for they will assist in this all important ministry of which I have commissioned you to conduct. These works cannot fail for it is what I want done for My glory and for the edification of My people to bring them closer to Me for conversion and salvation. I have called you out of the darkness and into My light and I charge you with the leadership of this work.

My Mother prays with you and watches over you and the others. Your perseverance, and that of My chosen little ones, are your signs of love and reverence for Me. Let no doubts hinder what I will do through you and My faithful.

(542-543) 5/24/93

(1st Healing Mass at St. Pius X Church)

Let all fall into place as I have planned. My work must be completed as time is waning. My Mother will be among you. She will be instrumental in what is about to take place this night. My light and peace falls upon those who come with expectation for relief of their problems, which encompass all phases of infirmity.

Be still and let My Spirit direct, as I heal according to My Will for their good. Lay your hands, give them My love, and pray for their well being.

All will flow, as My Spirit governs all the events that occur this night. You have but to be obedient and listen to My promptings, relayed through My Holy Spirit. Be at peace, My son, with those whom I have chosen to become an integral part of this ministry.

My people need healing.
My people need conversion.

Be the Balm of Gilead to them, as I give you My Spirit to lead you. I will do the rest! My Mother prays with you. Peace to all of you.

(563) 6/17/93

Give My love to those in ministry, as their prayers will increase the power to be bestowed upon My people.

(568) 6/25/93

I have given you what is needed for ministry, including powerful prayer warriors; therefore, go out in My Name and let My Will be done in My people. Be calm, be Me to My faithful.

(587) 7/26/93

My little children of this ministry overflow with dedication and commitment. If only more could follow their example. I have made a bond between you and they, a connection of spiritual love, if you will. Honor this merging of Christian love and the gifts and graces will flow abundantly. Concentrate with them, in ministry, and I will impart immense joy to all the members with the knowledge that all are participating in reaching souls that would not otherwise be attracted to the organized church. Go forward in boldness.

Pray for gifts! Pray for conversions! Pray for healings! My love to all of you. My peace to all of you.

(617-618) 9/8/93

Our Lady

On this special day, my son, I come to you and all who are gathered to give reverence to my Immaculate Heart, here in this place. Let my peace descend upon all of you and know that I, your heavenly Mother, loves each and every one of you.

My priest sons will be given their missions as you pray for them. Live with your sisters and brothers in my peace and in the peace of my Son, Jesus. You and all my cohort will be gifted for ministry. Be pleased that you and the others have been chosen, for it is a work of heaven to which service you have been called. Be united in your endeavors, so that the evil one cannot obtain a foothold in any of your lives.

You are children of the light and will be partakers of the Kingdom; therefore, take heart in all adversities, for it is the Will of my Son that you service Him in the conversion of souls. Come, all of you, under my Holy Mantle of protection and let us all go forward in the works of salvation.

(621) 9/12/93

Search your heart for answers which pertain to ministry. Is all being done to further the seeking out of souls for salvation? Opportunities will be apparent, but you and the others must capitalize upon them. Much work yet remains to be done as the days and the hours dwindle. Step out in the cause of faith and find the lost sheep.

(624) 9/15/93

These daughters whom I have handpicked are "holy warriors" of the final days. More may be added to their number, but know that they are fulfilling the missions that have been given them. You will all be clad with the armor of heavenly gifts, so that you may not be susceptible to the darts of the enemy. Be aware not of what is obvious danger, but what is insidious and unseen. Go in the peace of which is Our love!

(627) 9/19/93

I will bless all of you as you stand in the forefront to lead My people to conversion. Let all that I have taught you come to fruition in these times of dire need to bring the lost unto salvation. My Spirit will guide, My Spirit will open the doors, but you, My faithful, must cross the thresholds. Even if I leave doors only ajar, press on through. I need the dedication of prayerful, but forceful warriors, to fight the battle for souls. My rod and My staff will protect you as you go against the enemy in this conflict. Also, the mantle of My Mother will cover you, as well as My Precious Blood. Therefore, persevere as Paul, pray as Peter, and forge ahead allowing no quarter to the foe. Peace to you, My loved ones.

(634-635) 10/4/93

This message is of some urgency. Speak to the brothers and sisters. Although all of your problems seem to be overwhelming, the need to save souls must take precedence. Meet, pray and formulate a plan to enhance the ministry in new areas. I will open doors only if you will persevere in your endeavors in seeking to bring the sheep into the fold. My heart bleeds for the lost ones and I yearn to have them with Me for My Second Coming.

Go into the highways and the by-ways and gather My sheep. This is a commission that I have given you, My little ones, and it is with great hope and confidence that you will step out in faith and lead all whom you encounter, to conversion to My Sacred Heart. I will always be with each of you and My Holy Mother will pray with My little son, as he ministers to My people. Go, My children, in the knowledge that My Mother and I love you for your faithfulness to the Kingdom.

(655) 11/9/93

I will continue to direct you in ministry, along with the others. Persevere fervently to capture those souls who would otherwise be lost to perdition. I will open hearts as you persevere in faith as the battle ensues, to the last. Pray for direction and direction will be given. Pray for the gifts and they will be given. Pray for the lost souls and they will find Me.

(657) 11/21/93

Yes, no conversation has taken place as of late; however, the line of communication must remain open as My words are needed in ministry and in other areas. Be aware tomorrow, of possible problems, but none of which are unsolvable. Concentrate on prayer for My people. Call upon My Holy Spirit and, as always, leave the results to Me. I will renew them. I will console them. Tell the others that their efforts have not gone unnoticed as I have seen their perseverance for the Kingdom.

(691) 2/3/94

I will visit your heart as you strive to serve Me. Continue to obey and allow more teaching as to give furtherance to what I ask of you. Listen always to what I may reveal through the others for this is one of the ways in which you will receive revelation. I give you My Peace.

(695) 2/5/94

I am your Jesus, the one who sustains and protects you, as was shown you during your trials. Therefore, I ask of you, and My other children, more and deeper prayer so as to enhance all that I have given you to service the Kingdom.

(697-699) 2/11/94

You have no problem, except that which you create for yourself. All is progressing according to My Will. Persevere to seek and all will fit into place. Be cognizant of the fact that you will be used where you are most needed. Many will come to Me, through you, and through the others, who strive for witness to My Most Holy Name. There will be signs and the manifestations of gifts as the ministry is implemented in those places of which your are to pray.

I am continuing to build in this ministry, that which cannot be comprehended in your human terms. Question not, only obey as I lead you to various paths of which I will choose for ministry. All of you have been tested in the fire of My Divine Love, and through this purification, you will be used in the areas where there is the most need. My gifts follow you wherever you go and the fruits will be evident as your prayers will be heard by Me and My Holy Mother!

I send My love to this little flock, for their faith is so, that I am magnified to others because of their love for Me and My Mother. Be united and be in unison with My Sacred Heart and with the Immaculate Heart of My Mother and together we will bring souls to conversion and to salvation.

(701) 2/17/94

You will look to the events of which I am about to unfold. Pray for those who are in need at this time, whether they be few or many in number. Rely on your sisters, My little ones, who remain dedicated to My Sacred Heart and the Immaculate Heart of My Mother. Seek and you shall find lost souls.

(717) 3/22/94

In exchange for what you do for Me, I will grant you the grace to serve Me in greater capacity. I will pour out My gifts to you and the sisters. It will be by My Holy Spirit that you will manifest power to enhance the glory due Me. I bring you all My love and all My peace.

(718) 3/23/94

You will dispose of all that surrounds you that is not of Me. Use the means I have given you and know that its power comes from Me. You will know and understand more as the results become apparent. I will protect you and the others.

(726) 4/7/94

My answers are always direct, if you understand them. Go, and knock at the door. You will know if it is to be opened to you. Persevere and I will continue to work in the life of the ministry. Tell the brethren to put away all other distractions and pray for My people for that is the mission which I have given them.

(731) 4/16/94

You were told much the previous day of which you shared with your sisters. Recall to them all of which was said at that time. Know that I speak to My people through the gifts of which I bestow upon them.

(741) 5/9/94

Yes, this is where it all began for you, but not for Me. It began for Me on Calvary and now the legacy is left to My little ones to carry on the works I started 2000 years ago. Be encouraged, My son, for I will lead you, and the others in ministry, as I led My people of old with the cloud before them. You will all know the signs and the circumstances which will show you the way to access to My people who are in need of prayer for healing. I ask of you all: humility, perseverance, obedience and most of all, love. With these virtues, you will succeed in the mission I have given you. Be strong, and let not the evil one dissuade any of My little ones.

(762) 6/27/94

Pray for healing in general, as many will come away healed and converted. You will hear of these happenings at a later date. Know that through the power of My Holy Spirit that you have been used this night, to minister to My people. Remain little and let My presence overshadow all that will transpire. You will be the instrument I will use to free many from bondage. Listen always to Me as I instruct you from within. Listen always to your sisters as I instruct you through them also. Pray, fast and remain in a state of grace, so that you will be a clear vessel for My use in this ministry. I bless you, My son, and send you My peace.

(767) 7/12/94

I will call upon you shortly to endure more of what I may send you. Know that it will be for My Honor

and Glory and that I will use you further, in new
ways. I will bless you and all in the ministry, of
which you have been called to participate.

(773) 7/24/94

Your yes to Me was what I had waited for. It is what
began your life of service to Me. I will not restrict
your earthly life as long as you follow My precepts.
It is only in this service to Me that you will find true
peace. Relay this message to your sisters for it is My
word to them also.

(791) 8/25/94

There will be changes in ministry and you will adapt
to these changes. All will be for My Honor and Glory
and for the edification of My people. Continue to
obey My instructions and I will bless you, and the
others, in the Name of the Father and of the Son and
of the Holy Spirit.

(794-795) 8/29/94

During this quiet time with Me and the others, I will
relate what it is I want of all of you. It is My desire
that you come before Me and adore My Eucharistic
Heart and listen within your inner beings of where I
am leading each of you. Ask Me what it is you want
of Me and I will give it to you, if it be for your spiritual good and for My Honor and Glory. You will all
be blessed in ministry for I see the virtues of love,
compassion, humility and perseverance within each
of you. The works of this ministry must go on as this
mission is vital for the conversion and salvation of
many souls. I have created this ministry and will
have no one dismantle it. There may be alterations,
but the ministry will be. Listen always, as I direct
you with the still, inner voice and know that "I Am,

Who Am" will be with you in all that you do. MY
WORK WILL BE ACCOMPLISHED. I give My
love to you and to My other children.

(805) 9/17/94

Our Lady

As you place yourself before me on this holy ground,
I will bless you and my other children. All of you
have dedicated yourselves to ministry for which I am
pleased. Unite yourselves, even closer, in a circle,
back to back in protection of each other, and I will
be in the center of this circle, summoning legions of
angels to encircle and protect you. This circle will be
my circle of love of which I will always be a part.

Prepare for the onslaught as the evil one continues to
attempt to thwart the works of my Son. All has been
pre-ordained and my intervention will not allow
satan to touch a hair on your heads. My little ones, I
bless you in the Name of the Father and of the Son
and of the Holy Spirit.

(807-809) 9/23/94

Yes, as you call My Name, I speak to your heart
about many things. Recall the events of these past
three years, the anguish, loneliness and hurts of the
heart. My son, all this is for a purpose, so that you
would know of the burdens of My people for ministry to them and for the understanding of their
needs.

I do not desire the pious, I use wounded healers to
carry on My works. I will utilize each one of you,
My hand-chosen warriors, to become My voice, My
hands, My feet, My heart. I will fortify this ministry,
I will strengthen this ministry, until no one would
oppose you for they will see ME in this ministry of
love and compassion. Remain always as little chil-

dren awaiting the call of your Abba Father. Do My works as I direct you and not as you would have it. I have called all of you to summon My people and awaken them to the late hour that is upon them. If they abide in Me, I will abide in them, but the waning days are upon you and further extensions of My Merciful Heart are coming to an end. Work diligently as My Holy Spirit performs extraordinary feats through you. My new apostles, become My other Self to all whom you encounter, and the Doors of Heaven will welcome you in the Splendor of My glory.

(815) 10/3/94

You will receive what you need soon. I have brought you to the depths of despair so that you may perform acts of humility when necessary. I will not leave you orphaned, did you not know this? I will lift you up and thrust you forward, as My plan for you needs to be completed. I have given you others to uphold you and have molded them into this ministry, which was planned long ago. Be to everyone, Me, and I will fill your life with Us.

(816) 10/4/94

Stay in prayer each and every day, all through each and every day. Speak to Me daily. Let My Holy Spirit lift your spirit as you seek Me in all that you do and say, in My Name. I love you, My son. I love your sisters who are also My children. You please Me with your persevering spirits. I will deepen your prayer lives as you spend more time with Me in Holy Adoration and in doing the works for which you have been chosen.

Members of the Queen of Peace Healing Ministry
Front row - Angie Bator, Maria Maraschiello
Back row - Charlene McGraw, Joanne Wander
Recent Ministry Members:
Dominique Sanchez, Marianne Boccabella and Mary Weis.

Intercessory Prayer Group

STORY OF HER BANNER

The inspiration to create the "Queen of Peace Banner" began after I received a healing of migraine headaches when Tony laid hands and prayed over me. I then began to attend the healing masses of the Queen of Peace Healing Ministry at St. Pius X Church. It wasn't until I heard of the group's name that I received the inspiration for the banner. Other than love of quilting, and a fascination with stained glass windows, I have no artistic ability. But what I knew early on was that I wanted to do something to honor Our Lord and Our Lady.

I knew I wanted to use a stained glass effect, but since I am not an artist, I was looking for inspiration. At one of the healing masses at St. Pius X, in the fall of 2000, I happened to sit near the window that would become the pattern for the background. I took notes and made a sketch (yes, during mass), so that I would not forget the design! Construction began, and the piece took shape in its own time. Quilting was done by hand and machine. The doves and flowers are all hand sewn. The halo and mantle are hand sewn with gold and metallic thread. One of the layers of fabric used as the backbone of the project is linen that my grandmother made, in Italy, in the early 1900's. She actually made the threads from a flax plant, and wove them on a loom to make strips of cloth to be used for sheets, towels and clothing.

The first original layer (on the inside) is made from hand woven, hand spun fabric (linen) from Italy, made by my grandmother. This was used as a base for holding the additional pieces of fabric as they were arranged. I hung this on a wall, and pinned pieces of fabric on it. Often I would leave it up for several days, going back and rearranging as ideas came to me. The linen was made in the early 1900's by harvesting the stalks from flax plants, making the stalks into thread, and spinning the threads on a spinning wheel before going to the loom to be made into sheets or strips.

The second layer represents the "panes of glass" and the leading. The panes of glass were cut randomly, pinned on the backing and machine sewn. The black bias tape used as the

Our Lady's Banner
(Created by Anna Kraatz)

leading between the panes was machine sewn. Gold fabric netting was added over several of the panes, and hand quilted.

The third layer is the border (the window frame), which is also fabric from Italy, containing gold threads. This fabric covers the entire back of the wall hanging, and extends out on all four sides to form a window frame.

The fourth layer is the addition of the following materials and depictions:

The Queen of Peace with her solar halo (trimmed with gold cording and gold thread). The Queen of Peace is cut from a tapestry and hand stitched onto the "window". The halo is hand dyed fabric, and is trimmed in gold cording and quilted in gold thread. Her mantle, stitched with blue metallic thread. The doves (which are mosaics), with extra batting and quilted with gold thread. The flowers and the vines: the vines are machine sewn, the vines and flowers are hand sewn onto the window. The flowers have been enhanced with gold fabric paint. These were the last items to be added to the front.

The fifth layer is the quilted backing.

Construction on this project began in September 2000 and finished in April 2001. Much of the time involved in the process included having the wall hanging on a bedroom wall, adding and moving fabric and waiting for inspiration for the next layer or step. There was no planning involved in this project. I had no idea what the finished product would look like or what size it would be. Each day or week that went by gave me insight into what to do next. As I told you, I did not do this, this was divine inspiration, which brought me much joy and peace. I am honored to have been chosen to do this hand work.

Thank you,

Anna Kraatz

IN TESTIMONY

"I have already told you that a king's secret ought to be kept, but the things God does should be told to everyone...."

(Tobit 12:11)

"As Jesus made his way to Jerusalem, he went along the border between Samaria and Galilee. He was going into a village when he was met by ten men suffering from a dreaded skin disease. They stood at a distance and shouted, "Jesus! Master! Have pity on us!"

Jesus saw them and said to them, "Go and let the priests examine you." On the way they were made clean. When one of them saw that he was healed, he came back, praising God in a loud voice. He threw himself to the ground at Jesus' feet and thanked him. The man was a Samaritan. Jesus spoke up, "There were ten men who were healed; where are the other nine? Why is this foreigner the only one who came back to give thanks to God?" And Jesus said to him, "Get up and go; your faith has made you well."

(Luke 17: 11-19)

Some 2000 years ago, Jesus healed ten lepers; however only one returned to thank Him. It is the same today as it was then, only a small number come back to give witness of what God has done for them. But, the number of those who do come to tell us of their healings, continues to grow.

The following are testimonies of reported healings, some of which have been medically documented. I am not claiming these healings to be miracles, but only relating to what occurred. My mission is to fast, pray and lay on hands. I do not judge miracles.

In some of the testimonies that follow, only the initials of names have been used to protect the privacy of individuals.

Rev. Joseph Bertha, PhD

9/25/00

When Tony laid hands on my shoulders, I did not know what to expect. As I stood, I opened my eyes, then he began to pray. Some moments into the prayer, Tony looked me in the eyes and said that I should close my eyes, which I did. As soon as I closed them, I saw the image of the face of the Shroud of Turin/Veronica's Veil, in white lines, the positive version of a photographic negative. This image brought great peace and calm into my soul, I felt rested and at ease.

I believe that the face cloth, Veronica's Veil, that I saw, is the face veil from the Shroud of Turin. What a beautiful irony; My Grandmother, Mother and Sister all have the same name "Veronica" – Vera- i- kona; true icon, true image.

Rev. Joseph Bertha, PhD

3/13/01

On another occasion Tony prayed over me. During this session, I first saw streams of Korean writing. This vision was confirmed later that evening as someone brought up the instance of a non-Catholic Korean flying to the U.S. and being reunited with a Catholic friend, for possible conversion. I also saw a statue of the Virgin Mary; she was dressed in white with a blue sash, she was crying. Two other manifestations were of a stream of stars and a blue colored cathedral rose window.

Father Bertha has been appearing on EWTN Global Catholic Television, on many occasions speaking about Icons of the Annunciation, Evangelization, and the Eastern Catholic Churches.

Sr. Emma Carsten

I'm a Franciscan Sister of St. Joseph from Hamburg, New York. I used to work in the field of health care at Our Mother House. Our retired Senior Sisters were a joy to work with.

For about 13 years I suffered migraine headaches. In the beginning, I experienced about two migraines a year but as time passed, they increased in number and intensity. I'll never forget the pain and frustration, the stomach upsets, and the inability to take even one step without magnifying the throbbing pain. It was difficult to minister to the Sisters when I was confined to bed for three days at a time, completely helpless.

On July 29, 1995, two Sisters from my convent treated me to a trip to Marmora, Canada. We traveled by bus with a group from Orchard Park, New York. After making the outdoor Stations of the Cross, our group leader announced that Tony Cubello, a person in the Healing Ministry, was willing to lay hands on all those who wished to step forward. I stood back, watching and wondering who this guy was who prayed over people. I was used to seeing a priest in that role. Finally, thinking of my migraines, I decided to step forward. I felt a gust of wind and the next thing I knew I was on the ground unable to get up. I experienced peace, a most beautiful feeling of peace. Also, I felt heat all around my head and face and I saw lights flashing all around me.

Would you believe it? I haven't had a migraine since. Praise the Lord!!!

Besides the migraines, I used to suffer from frequent severe sinus headaches. Since I have been attending the Healing Masses at St. Pius X, the sinus headaches have practically disappeared. I've really been blessed for I can function much better physically, mentally, and spiritually without headaches.

Colleen Williams

2/22/98

The other day I received a call from a woman that I had never met. She asked me if I had ever spoken with Tony. At first I thought she (like I had been) was a bit skeptical about coming to the healing mass, and was looking to me to offer some hope that indeed anything was possible. She asked me to relay my story to her. Without questioning her as to her reason for the call, I found myself telling this complete stranger about a very personal experience. One that, well — to be perfectly honest — I hadn't thought about for several months and had only told a few of my friends and family. In fact, for a long time after it had happened I had looked for and expected some revelation that would offer me insight as to why this had happened to me. Why God had chosen to touch me in such a special way. As I spoke to this woman, it hit me. In that one brief moment it suddenly made sense. Perhaps I was healed in order that I could give testimony to the healing power of the Holy Spirit. She asked me to come and talk with you. I could not refuse.

My story begins Christmas Day 1996. For several weeks I hadn't been feeling well. I chalked it up to the stress of the holidays. I am a professional singer and had been keeping a very hectic schedule in addition to caring for family. But when I woke up Christmas morning, I discovered a large, painful lump on my neck. I had been having difficulty swallowing and experienced some pain when I would perform. Needless to say, anything that might prevent me from performing caused me great anxiety. With each new blood test, ultrasound, scan, the picture looked bleaker and bleaker. It was determined by three physicians and a surgeon that I had thyroid cancer. Typically, this is a very treatable illness in women. But frankly, this was a club of which I did not want to be a member. Those of you here, who have ever received a cancer diagnosis, know that no matter what your chances are of beating it, the idea that you might be facing death is overwhelming. Despite your best efforts, it's very difficult to keep a positive outlook. Regretfully, my doctors told me that while they believed the cancer to be treatable, it was aggressive, and so I was facing not only immediate surgery but also a course of chemo and radiation. And then...well...they just said we would have to wait and see...

On the day before the final consultation with the surgeon, I awoke to read the morning edition of the *Buffalo News*. In it was a review of my Friday evening performance. It was glowing, but instead of basking in the glory of a job well done, I was despondent. I saw it as a bad omen. This was my fifteen minutes of fame. Not only would I never sing again, but I was convinced I was going to die. And the thought of leaving my three children behind was more than I could bear. And then I received a phone call from my friend Ellen. She said she had been praying for me and for some reason had this overwhelming need to call me and tell me about the healing mass here at St. Pius X. I told her I appreciated the thought, but that I wasn't sure that I was comfortable with the whole idea, and I doubted, that even if it were possible, that I was worthy of such a gift. Still I was compelled to go.

Scared and overwhelmed I came to the church that night as you have this evening. Wanting to be healed, but truly believing that I wasn't deserving. In fact, that evening I prayed not to be cured but rather to be given the courage and the strength to face this ordeal. The priest spoke about forgiveness, about letting go of the anger and the hurt. Only by truly forgiving could you be open to the healing power of the Holy Spirit. I'm ashamed to say, there is an individual who I had never been able to forgive. In fact, a person I truly despised. In that moment, I realized that I had to let that go. None of that mattered anymore.

I watched as others went up to the altar. I remember literally shaking; I was terrified. I'm not sure what was more frightening to me, the possibility that nothing would happen or that something might. I stood in the line until Tony approached me. He looked at me and chuckled, and then took my hand and said, "You are so nervous, relax, what do you think I'm going to do to you?" I had wanted to say, "Cure me", but I simply said sheepishly, "I don't know". He didn't ask what had brought me there and I didn't offer. He made the sign of the cross on my forehead and then put his hands around my throat, not on the shoulder or the hand or head as he had with the others before me. For some reason, I immediately closed my eyes and I instantly felt this rush of heat on my face. I saw a flash of light from right to left and then suddenly I could feel myself falling. I fought it because I didn't want to appear foolish. But such a feeling overcame me, and before I knew what was happening I found myself flat on my back at the front of the altar. My God, what had just happened to me? I went back to my seat and cried quietly for several minutes. When I stopped, I simply got up and went home. Driving home, I felt such a tremendous sense of peace. I knew that no matter what happened, in God's plan, I would be able to face it.

The news the next day was even more distressing. The doctor's had discovered that surgery at this point would be very risky due to my very elevated heart rate and blood pressure, functions of the diseased thyroid. Surgery would have to wait until an endocrinologist could regulate the thyroid. Through all of the discussions that morning, however, I remained calm, almost resigned. I was scheduled in the afternoon with the endocrinologist. After a very thorough physical exam, and after he had evaluated the barrage of tests and scans, this doctor concluded that I did not have cancer. In fact, I didn't have any tumor at all, and surgery was certainly not necessary. I sat there in complete disbelief. How could so many have been wrong? How could such a mistake have been made? My illness, he said, was merely an inflammatory disease, treatable with medication. Certainly, I would continue to be monitored, but he said to me "Go! Live life!"

Some would call this a gross error in judgment, nothing more than a case of medical malpractice. Others would say that I was given a reprieve. Some would say I was touched by the Holy Spirit.

In the months that followed, you would think that I would have been flying high. I was cancer free. Still I fell into a deep depression. Somehow facing my mortality made me see how unhappy I was in my life, how empty I felt inside. Finally, unable to live this way, wallowing in my own self-pity, I came to the realization that the power was within me. I was responsible for my own happiness. I had to stop complaining and blaming. I had to start forgiving not only others but myself as well. I made the choice to change my life, to become empowered. And in doing that, I have taken this second chance that God has given me and have become a better mother, a better friend.

We will never know if I was truly healed in the physical sense by the power of the Holy Spirit, but still I am grateful; for this experience changed my life emotionally and spiritually in ways that I'm only now beginning to realize, and for reasons I may not ever truly understand.

Sr. Rosemary

Mr. Tony Cubello prayed with me at the Healing Mass at Our Lady of Lourdes Church, Rochester, New York, on October 29, 2001. As I waited in line, I had an awareness that I would be "slain in the Spirit." I was prayed with briefly before I went down. I had tried to approach this prayer time with an open heart. I had prayed during the Mass for some areas of my life that needed God's grace, and did not specifically ask for one particular thing as I was prayed with, knowing that God knew what was best.

I felt very calm and peace-filled as I laid on the floor. Once I stood up and walked back to my pew, I realized more and more, that as I walked, both my legs' hamstrings had been touched in a special way. As a runner, I had sore hamstrings that gave me discomfort on a regular basis. That pain and soreness was now gone! The next morning, I went out running and did not experience any of my usual discomfort, in fact I ran seven miles! I have been running ever since, with some normal hamstring discomfort, but not with the intensity of the pain I had before I attended that Healing Mass.

Sister Rosemary was one of more than 7,000 people throughout the country chosen to carry the Olympic flame, being passed from torch to torch, across the United States to Salt Lake City for the opening ceremonies of the February 2002 Olympic Games.

Carol Ferro

I would like to take this time to thank our Lord Jesus for a healing I received this past year. It was a year ago, April of 1999 that a large mass was discovered in my breast. I had to go for several sonograms, at three month intervals. The mass had grown considerably between April and July and after being examined further it was decided that I should have a biopsy of the tumor. I was scheduled for the biopsy in November of 1999.

I attended a healing mass, here at St. Pius X, and was prayed over by Tony. In addition to that night of prayer, I had a private session of prayer again, with the laying on of hands. At that time, I experienced a sensation of warmth in my afflicted area. I went for the scheduled biopsy in November but was told that I should have another mammogram first. Upon doing so, the mammogram showed there was no longer any tumor present. A second mammogram was taken and the doctor was simply stunned, and smilingly said, "I'm very puzzled, everything is absolutely normal, you don't need the biopsy and I don't need to see you for another year.

Documentation of both reports are presently available.

Carol Ferro (Brother's Healing)

12/17/00

My name is Carol Ferro and I would like to share with you this night the healing that my brother Frank has had.

After extensive testing by two different radiologists, my brother Frank was diagnosed in July of 2000 with cancer of the voice box and the tongue. I asked Tony for prayer for him. We had entered the hospital and a biopsy was done on him, which also confirmed the diagnosis of the two radiologists. He was taken into surgery about 3 weeks later. They were actually contemplating removal of the larynx and they removed a lot of the growth and a sac; miraculously, it turned out to be non-malignant. And, of course, they didn't have to proceed with the voice box removal, praise God. We are very grateful to Tony and his ministry for all the prayers and the positive results we obtained.

One more detail, they had actually started my brother on a round of chemotherapy and radiation. They showed us a film on the electronic voice box they were going to be implanting in him. In their minds there was an absolute certainty of this malignancy, which as I said, turned out miraculously negative. They were, to say the least, shocked! They were absolutely stunned at these findings that turned up after he was prayed for. All I can say is: thank the good Lord, and for the intercession of the Blessed Mother and Tony's prayers with the ministry, we are forever grateful. Thank You.

Mary Ann Wunsch

I would like to say that we first came to St. Pius X Church for the healing mass on April 24th because my granddaughter, Haylee, was diagnosed legally blind. Her optic nerve never fully developed. This baby is very special. She has brought much love to our family and people she comes in contact with.

Tony Cubello said before he was to pray over the people, that Jesus told him specific things that would need special prayer. One of them was for a problem with the eyes and vision. We were so happy.

On May 2nd, Tuesday evening, Tony and the Queen of Peace Healing Ministry came to my daughter's apartment. We invited family and friends to come pray for my granddaughter. It was a most loving and moving experience. When Tony was praying over the baby, my aunt said she saw God the Father take the baby in His arms and cradle her and lightly breathe his breath on her. You could feel the power of the Holy Spirit in the apartment.

He proceeded to pray over each of us individually. Another aunt in attendance had an accident a few years ago and she had whip lash. She would have ringing in her ears and pain on the side of her neck. After Tony prayed over her, her ears turned bright red like a bad sunburn and were hot. I talked to her on Wednesday evening the 17th of May and she hasn't had any recurrence of pain or ringing in her ears.

One more thing that I would like to share is that on Monday, May 1st, we went to the healing mass at St. Margaret's Church in Buffalo, where the Queen of Peace Healing Ministry was conducting a healing service. Tony said that someone needed to make a huge decision (that was me). I asked the next night at my daughter's when everyone was there for our healing service to pray that I make my decision. On May 7th I made my decision through the grace of God, Jesus, the Holy Spirit and Our Blessed Mother's help. Praise the Lord! Something I learned is LOVE; the love of the Lord is so powerful, it will make you complete, happy and joyful. Another thing is to forgive. To forgive anything of your past or present. Also, to forgive yourself is a healing in itself. If you can't forgive, sometimes it impedes your healing process. So take all the love and forgiveness you can hold in your heart and soul and thank Jesus for all the wonderful things in your life even if it seems hopeless. Have faith, Jesus won't let go of you.

I thank you Jesus, and Tony Cubello and the Queen of Peace Healing Ministry for coming into our lives.

Hynda Zabel

01-17-01

Tony,

I just wanted to tell you a little bit about my mom since you saw her last. As you recall, my family and I placed a call to you and your ministry from St.Pius X asking if you would come to Millard Fillmore Hospital and lay hands on my mother who was critically ill.

A few weeks earlier, after minor elective outpatient surgery, the level of oxygen in her blood had plummeted, her lungs had filled with fluid and infection and she had lapsed into a coma, without warning and without explanation. Doctors gave her little chance of survival. We were, in fact, told that she had less than a 5% chance of making it. We had consulted countless numbers of doctors and had seemingly exhausted all medical hope. We even experimented with holistic methods of healing. Throughout it all, of course, we had prayed, all to no avail. Then we heard about you.

Being brought up in the Jewish faith, my family and I hesitated before making the call, but then decided that G-d is G-d and praying is praying. At that point, we were willing to try anything. I must say we were all more than a bit skeptical at first, but our thoughts changed quickly. While you were there, we watched the monitors mounted above my mothers head (showing her vital signs) begin to improve right before our eyes. Within a few days, my mother began to grow stronger and stronger. And two weeks later, the same woman who had suddenly lapsed into a ten week coma with little hope for survival was just as suddenly coming out of it!

The only thing that we can attribute her recovery to is your visit, her strong spirit, a loving and dedicated family and a lot of praying, especially yours!!!

Three months after emerging from her coma, my mother celebrated her birthday. She stood in a local restaurant surrounded by the doctors and nurses who cared for her, friends from across the country and her family, all of us looking on with tears in our eyes. She even danced with my father!

In the year and a half that has passed, my mother has never asked much about her illness, a bit scared I think to know too much. But I have noticed that my parents have rejoined our community temple, and once again are emphasizing the importance of religion and faith to their children and grandchildren. I know I not only speak for myself, but for each of us who stood vigil 24-hours-a-day, seven-days-a-week, at my mother's side throughout her illness and her recovery. We know that there was something much stronger than medicine that healed her, that helped all of us get through this.

Thank you for opening your hearts and minds, and for sharing your gift with us. I promised myself that I would spread the word to anyone I know about our miraculous experience. I hope our story will enable others to restore their hope, strengthen their faith and take comfort in the knowledge that there is a G-d and that you need to hold him in your heart.

I have since shared this experience with many of my friends who have been in need of some "holy intervention". I know that they too will share my experience.

Thank you and G-d Bless.

Lynn Sheer

For many years I had been involved in new age teachings and it took a toll on my health and my emotions. In 1989, my eye doctor retired me due to severe eye problems, namely a cataract, glaucoma, and a partially detached retina. Also, at this time, I was fighting addictions to cigarettes, marijuana and cocaine.

In 1994, I started attending the healing masses at St. Pius X Catholic Church in Getzville, New York. I am a convert to this faith. I had been attending healing masses for visual problems as well as problems with addiction. After attending the healing masses, I lost all addictions as well as gained more vision than I ever had. I attribute this to the Grace of God and being told about the healing masses at St. Pius X.

I was blessed to be introduced to Mr. Anthony Cubello in the summer of 1994 and attended his healing masses from 1994 through 1995. When I come to Buffalo for a visit I attend the healing masses whenever possible.

Peggy O'Connor

March 2001

After it was discovered that I had a brain tumor the size of a softball behind my right eye, which the doctors said was growing for several years and had made me blind in my right eye, I was immediately admitted to the hospital for surgery. The day before the surgery, my friend called and asked me if the ministry she was a part of could come and pray with me. I said sure thinking, at that point, I'll take all the help I can get. That night they arrived and Tony Cubello laid hands on me while the rest of them stood around my bed and prayed. While resting in the Spirit, I saw a very bright light and then felt a peace I have never felt before. The next day my family were all crying as they wheeled me into surgery, but I still felt that peace and was certain that I was going to be fine. This was even after the doctors told us of all the side effects I could have, such as not recognizing anyone upon waking up from the surgery.

However, after coming out of a 10-1/2 hr. surgery, I recognized everyone and felt no pain after being cut from ear to ear. I believe I had a miracle and God had healed me and the instrument He used for my healing was Tony.

I thank God for His love and mercy and ask all to believe in the power of prayer, according to the Divine Will of God.

Jeffrey Baughan

1/28/99

I would like to speak to you about two healings that I have witnessed over the past several months. The first healing was a physical healing of my 5 year-old daughter; the second was a spiritual healing of myself that gave me the strength to endure the journey with my daughter and family.

EVENTS:

My daughter had been sick for a year and a half. In February of 1998, unknowingly she aspirated a piece of food into her lung. Following that she had several bouts of reoccurring pneumonia, which the doctors could not explain. She was in and out of the hospital several times for x-rays, Cat Scans and an MRI. She had two extended stays at the hospital for two procedures where a surgeon went into her lung and removed plugs of infection and mucus. We had progressed from her pediatrician to an infectious disease specialist, then a surgeon and finally to a lung specialist. At every juncture, the doctors did not know what was going on with her and moved us on to another specialist. Throughout this time, my daughter was quite ill, medicated for one and a half years and we were unsure of where to turn.

She became very ill again in November 1998 and another CT scan was scheduled. The results of the CT scan indicated that there was a mass on her lung and that her lung had collapsed. The doctors were still unsure of what it was and what the next step should be. The doctors kept her on an antibiotic throughout this period.

In November of 1998, I started attending the healing mass with my daughter. I also started attending daily mass and praying for wisdom and strength to go on. We continued attending the healing mass and receiving the blessing. At the end of March, we took her off the medication and she was well for 8 days before getting ill again. A CT scan in March indicated that the mass was still there. We had an MRI scheduled in April but it was delayed because she was sick. The MRI was rescheduled for June. Our meeting with the doctors to review the MRI results was delayed an additional week due to scheduling.

Finally, we had our discussion with the doctor and we were notified that "the area is considerably smaller", additionally, no surgery was required and that we were to remove her from the medication. We were informed that "the area is scar tissue" and the doctors were no longer concerned.

My daughter has been fine. I give witness that my daughter has been healed and I have received the strength to support her and my family through our journey. Thank You.

Mark Lettieri

10-23-00

As you listen to my testimony, I hope you'll take it to heart, because it comes from my heart. As some of you already know, I became paralyzed from the chest-down in an auto accident on July 12, 1996, a little more than four years ago. I was thrown through the open sunroof of my car, while it was doing flips. I was not wearing a seat belt then, but I do now! I had to learn the hard way, not only to wear my seat belt but to learn of God's presence and love in my life and all of our lives.

God was always telling me things, like to slow down and not to worry, but I was just too busy trying to get ahead in life, I simply was not listening to Him. He even gave me a premonition that I would end up one day in a wheelchair, and how I should behave while in it. "Be happy" was His message, there is a lot more to life than money, and being able to walk. Well, I ignored

God, and I went on with my busy and worrying way of life.

I also remember, shortly before my accident, Mother Teresa said on TV: "Suffering is a kiss from God." I was baffled why Mother Teresa would say this. I admired and respected Mother Teresa greatly; but I thought, how could anyone say that suffering is a kiss from God? The answer to this question will come later, after I explain more details of my story.

So then, the accident occurred. While in the hospital for three months, just lying there, it finally gave me the opportunity and time to listen to God. He told me to rest and I had to listen to Him! He told me not to ever worry, that everything would be taken care of. God filled me with His joy and peace. This joy and peace was so awesome, that I cannot describe it with words!

After my stay in the hospital and rehabilitation, I had to get back into the swing of things of this world, like taking care of family and work, etc. I found God's joy and peace in me greatly diminishing, because of worldly pressures, and me losing my focus on God, again.

But then I had the privilege to attend my first Healing Mass here, I mostly cried. But my crying was good because God shared it. The presence of the Holy Spirit was tremendous; I could feel it. Gifted Tony Cubello did the laying on of hands, and I felt God's peace once again! I was thirsty for this peace, so I continued attending these Healing Masses at St. Pius X Church. I believe it was either the first or second one, when a now dear friend, gave her healing testimony. She proclaimed that reciting and meditating on the Rosary every day gave her so much blessing and comfort. I've been growing in my prayer life, and because of what my friend said, I felt led to follow her example of praying the Gospels in my everyday life. Hence, these Healing Masses have touched me and brought me into a much deeper prayer life. God has blessed others and me because of my prayers. God answers prayers said from the heart, and in believing faith. God is truly wonderful and we have become very close. I am not driven by money anymore; God drives me.

My wife, I know prays for me to walk. She has questioned

me on how I was praying, because she expected me to walk by now, because of my Faith. It was by her questions that I realized that I wasn't praying so much for me to walk, but to get back the joy and peace from God that I had when I was lying on my back in that hospital room for three months. Glory to God, I have gotten the joy and peace back, in my mind, body, and soul!

Now, God is telling me through Tony and others, not to tolerate anything I want changed. And that's exactly what I have been doing with myself in this wheelchair. I have been tolerating it. I had accepted my suffering, offering it up to God, and simply living one day at a time. Tony would always tell me that God's healing comes from faith and having the right attitude for change and to be persistent in my prayers. So God is not done with me yet. He has been healing me from the inside out! I am truly a much better person today, than I was before my accident. Even though I can't walk, I have learned to change my attitude and not to tolerate the fact that I can't walk. But I especially pray for me to grow in faith and love of God. And of course, I will continue praying for all of you.

In closing, I guess Mother Teresa was right. Being paralyzed has truly been a wonderful grace from God "a kiss from God". It has been said, valleys are not to live in, they are to learn in. I have been blessed with a lot of good learning.

As so many before me have had added to my life in similar ways, I hope by God's grace, I've added to yours, even in some small way. God bless you all.

Angela Saviano

3/23/98

There are no small miracles, only miracles, and they have happened to me.

One month ago today, February 23, 1998, I was told that I had 2 lumps on my breast, and the breast would have to be removed and followed up with radiation and chemotherapy. This would have to be confirmed with a biopsy.

177

I drove home and called my friends for support. How blessed I am to have them. Nancy asked if I would be open to a healing prayer session at her home. I had been to one two years ago, I said yes. My mind, body and spirit thought they knew the power of prayer.

On March 1st, I went to a small private healing service. My friend, Nancy, invited everyone that wanted to be there, so I was surrounded by loving prayerful people. I was to have the biopsy the next day.

When Tony prayed over me and laid his hands on me, I fell with ease to the floor. My body was turbulent, it seemed there was something in me that wanted out, I believe it was the cancer, and it was like a volcano when it erupted and left. I was still and calm and stuck to the floor "in peace". I have been in peace through all this and have remained in peace, calm and spirit filled, from that point on.

This renewed strength opened the door for Jesus and Mary to do their work. How easy it became, I walk with them when I get off the mental track. I ask them to put me back on track and Jesus and Mary never, never refused!!

On March 2, the biopsy was done in a room that was wallpapered with ROSES. On March 5 the doctor called. One lump was malignant and one was benign. His words to me were "this is good news". A lumpectomy not a mastectomy would be done. My words for this are " A Miracle".

The lump showed two centimeters on the mammogram, my family was told. May God bless them for their support. Surgery was scheduled for March 17, St. Patrick's Day! On March 16, 1998, I attended another healing mass. When I went into surgery, I was calm and peaceful. I envisioned Jesus and Mary wheeling me in holding my hands; I prayed that they let this be pain free and that I would wake up healthy.

Our prayers were answered, I woke up pain free and I have been pain free!!

The lump was only 8mm, not 2cm. I asked the doctor what he thought about that, and he responded by asking what I thought, I said "I know this was prayers answered."

He never discounted my answer, he just had a smile on his face. (You see I know Jesus sent me to him). "Another Miracle". He (the doctor) told me that this is the best news, that all the reports point to the very best prognosis for a healthy life.

So I know there is power in the "laying on of hands" and I know that Miracles happen today and every day, they are happening to me.

Robert Gugino

I have been attending these healing masses for the past six years, after a diagnosis of bladder cancer, for which I was prayed over at St. Pius X Church for the past six years. During my annual check up with my physician I was found to be cancer free. My doctor was amazed and curious as to how this could be. Until this point I was still smoking cigarettes on a daily basis, which the doctor related as the main cause of my bladder cancer. About two years ago, Tony approached me at the healing mass that I attended to convince me that I had to realize my own problem with smoking. Tony called upon the Holy Spirit to help give me the strength and conviction to help me stop smoking. On April 20th, 1998, I went to have a chest x-ray and the technician told me not to get dressed because he may need to take another film. After reviewing the film it showed some cloudiness; the technician took another x-ray. Ten days later I was at the doctors office. I asked the doctor what the results were. I was informed that the films were clear, that there was no problem at all.

That day that I walked out of the x-ray office. Crossing the parking lot, I reached for one more cigarette but could not seem to be able to light it. I feel that the Holy Spirit waited for this moment to give me the wake-up call to quit. After smoking at least one pack of cigarettes a day for the last 55 years, I am now smoke free. I know that Tony is not the healer; but with the encouragement of Tony and all my dear friends in the prayer groups, I was guided to the Holy Spirit to seek the help that I needed. All I can say at this time is "thank you" to my dear friends, but most of all, THANK YOU to the LORD. Praise the Lord!

Laurette Irwin

Good evening. My name is Laurette. I'm here because I promised the good Lord that I would be a witness to Him for the healing He has given me. I want to be one of the ten people to come back and thank Him. As soon as people get what they want, they forget about God until the next time they need Him. Well, that's wrong. We should give praise and thanks to our Lord everyday of our lives.

Anyway, two years ago I was diagnosed with breast cancer. I was terrified just hearing the word "cancer" alone is frightening. I had an open biopsy done at the hospital, so I had to wait for the results. A week later, my husband and I went to the doctor's office to get the results. The doctor walked in and said, "Yes, you have cancer", just like that. I was in shock. Did we hear him right? He must have made a mistake, but he said it again. Then the doctor left us alone in the office. My husband hugged me and we both began to cry. Then he said to me, "Laurette, I truly love you and I will never leave your side. I'm with you whatever happens."

A few days later we went to a surgeon. He really thought it had spread to my lymph nodes. He told me it would be a terrible year; radiation, chemo, etc.. The kind of surgery was up to me. My husband and I prayed on it, so I called and told him I decided to have a mastectomy. The surgery was scheduled for Tuesday, October 10 at 10:00 AM.

The night before my surgery, Tony Cubello and the Queen of Peace Ministry came to my house to pray over me. My cousin gave me his name and phone number. He had prayed over some people she knew and many miracles occurred. After he prayed over me, I rested in the Spirit. I felt a fluttering feeling in my breast. After they left, I felt a peaceful feeling I can't explain. I got up early the next day, went to mass, so I was ready to go to the hospital. The fear all went away.

Thank God the surgery went well. I was still at peace that whole night. The next morning the doctor came in and told me I would get my results by Monday. They sent me home. The next morning nobody could tell I had surgery. I was walking around like nothing happened. I know it was all the prayers.

Thursday morning when I got up I saw this bright light in my bedroom mirror. I remember saying to myself, "It's the light of God and He's going to heal me". Around 12:00 I started to feel kind of tired, so I laid on the couch for three hours. I couldn't get myself up. I wasn't sleeping, just out of it. It was the same feeling I have when I rested in the Spirit. I could hear voices, everything going on, but I just couldn't function. My husband made me lunch. I dragged myself to the table and I just couldn't eat. My head just fell over. I had to lie down. My husband got worried. He kept asking me what's wrong. I could hardly talk, but very slowly and softly I kept repeating that the Holy Spirit is healing me. When my boys came home form school, I heard them saying, "Mom, what's wrong?" I think my husband finally understood what was going on, so he explained this to the kids. All of a sudden around 3:00 PM, the "Hour of Mercy", I became alert. It was strange, I was wide awake and very much at peace.

Around 3:30 PM the phone rang. It was the doctor. I was shaking. He said "good news" the cancer did not spread. You are cancer free." If only you could hear me, mind you now, I'm still on the phone with the doctor. I yelled out "Praise be Jesus, Thank You Jesus", and I couldn't stop crying and thanking God. Then it hit me after I hung up, did I hear him correctly? But he told my husband the same thing.

The following week I saw the doctor at his office. He said to me "I didn't want to scare you, but I was certain it spread; I can't believe it." I said "I do." and I held up my rosary. I said "It was God that helped me." He said, "You don't need any radiation or chemo. You are cancer free."

I can never praise and thank God enough for all that he has done for me. Not only did the good Lord heal me, but also, he had my brothers and sisters pray so much. We get together so many times to pray. It was so awesome to see everybody praying together.

So remember, Pray, Pray, Pray,

Never stop praying.

That's all we have is God!

Mary Weis

In 1995 my life seemed to be in total turmoil. I remember driving home one night, crying and asking God to help me find some direction. I felt alone and it was an intense loneliness even though I was married and had two children. The next day I was scheduled to go for a mammogram and a malignant tumor was found in my breast. I had a mastectomy, and within a couple of weeks I was having chemotherapy. As a side effect of the surgery, I developed lymphedema (swelling) in my right hand and arm.

I grew up in an Italian, Catholic religious family. After going off to college and marrying a non-Christian, my religion had seemed to lose its importance in my life. I attended mass on occasion and hadn't been to confession in years. A couple of Sundays after my surgery I felt a desire to go to church. The priest announced that during the week there would be a mass with the "laying on of hands". I assumed that "laying on of hands" was probably similar to blessing of the throat. With my hand and arm being swollen as a result of the surgery, I thought it would be a good idea to have my hand blessed. My mom came to the mass with me. After mass, people started coming up to the altar and Tony was putting his hands on people's heads and they started falling on the floor. My mom and I looked at one another and wondered what we had gotten into. Little did I know, at the time, that this was the beginning of God answering my prayer for help. God directed me to this healing ministry for prayer, guidance, and direction back to the Lord. Neither my mom nor myself "rested in the Spirit" that night. When Tony got done praying he asked if anyone wanted special prayer at their seat. My mom raised her hand and pointed to me. The ministry came over and gave us special prayer. We started crying, but then felt a special feeling of calmness that was very hard to explain in words. I had been touched by the Holy Spirit, but at the time didn't understand what had happened. The next time the healing ministry prayed over me I "rested in the Spirit" with my body trembling all over. Again, I was still confused about what was happening, but certain that I was being touched.

I have been to the monthly healing masses every month since. I know God answered my prayers. Through the healing ministry he has given me a spiritual healing with prayer and guidance and understanding. I no longer feel lonely; I have my best friend back, God.

Diane Carpino

01/07/02

I have never really done any public speaking, but this miracle just has to be shared. I had gone for a yearly physical in May 2001. Afterwards, my doctor called to tell me that my white blood cell count was elevated. He wanted me to wait a month and then retake a blood test. I was feeling just fine, no sickness or symptoms of anything being wrong. In June, after more blood work, the test showed my white blood cell level had gone down but was still not at a normal level. Waiting another three weeks for yet another blood test, the results showed that the white count had elevated higher than the very first test. At this point in time, I still was feeling fine. My doctor then sent me to a hematologist and explained that the first thing he was going to do was test me for a form of Leukemia. As it turns out, Leukemia was ruled out. With my white blood count going higher and after a series of tests and CT scans, what showed itself was some suspicious lymph nodes near the bottom of my trachea tube and several in my chest near my heart. This suggested that I might have some form of Lymphoma. Surgery was the next step to remove and biopsy these concerning nodes. Once there was a diagnosis, I would then be treated. I was scheduled for surgery on Friday, November 30. On November 26, I came to St. Pius X and attended a healing mass, which I have attended many times.

When Tony prayed over me and I was resting in the Spirit, I felt a warm feeling in my chest, a feeling I have never felt before. At first, I thought it was my imagination so I paid close attention to it. The feeling was nothing very powerful but there was definitely a very light warm feeling. I then went for my surgery four days later. The diagnosis after surgery that was given to me was that I had some calcified lymph nodes, which were removed, and there was no sign of any Lymphoma like originally suspected. When I had my follow-up with my surgeon, his exact words to me were that it was a "mystery" as to what had taken place in my body and why I had calcified lymph nodes. I had told him about the healing mass that I attended and he looked at me without any hesitation and said that he too believed the effects of the healing mass. He looked at my daughter who was with me and said, "you take that with faith also and believe that," and she does. I have been blessed and I thank Our Heavenly Father.

Richard Teetsel

I just know that I wanted to write to thank you and your entire team for the wonderful work you are doing. My wife, Sarah, and I have attended two recent healing masses at St. Edmund's and St. Pius X, in prayerful hope and faith for the healing of her cancer. She has felt touched at both masses and believes she is being healed. I too, have felt our Lord's presence and healing power at these masses.

A brief bit of medical information: Sarah developed breast cancer in 1997 and had a mastectomy, followed by chemotherapy. In 2000, the breast cancer reappeared in her right lung and she began weekly chemotherapy again, which shrunk and controlled the cancer. Still, in January of this year, she had to have urgent brain surgery for a malignant tumor there, and then three weeks of radiation treatments to try to eliminate two spots that couldn't be safely reached with the surgeon's knife.

Follow-up MRI after the mass at St. Pius X showed that the two spots have shrunk dramatically and she is getting stronger. We believe that the masses, as well as good medical care, are working to make her well.

We want to thank you and your team for using your gift of healing (1 Corinthians 12:28) to heal so many. We think the ladies who spoke at St. Pius X, especially the one who gave such strong assurance that Christ was present with us, and the faithful "catchers" who accompany you on you healing mission all do wonderful work.

We pray that God continues to bless you in your healing ministry!

P.D.

11/25/98

I'm 36 years old and was diagnosed with Tourettes syndrome in 1995. Tourettes syndrome is a neurological disorder that is genetically inherited. When I was first diagnosed in 1995 my "tics" (uncontrolled movements), were very mild and I didn't take the medication prescribed because of the harsh side effects.

Last year, in October of 1997, my Tourettes syndrome became worse overnight. I woke up one morning with severe body tremors, uncontrollable movements of my head and arms; and was constantly dropping things or falling due to the shaking. Since then I had increased sensitivity to loud noises and stimuli which made my motor symptoms (tics) worse. I often had to wear earplugs to decrease the stimuli. I had the following "tics" associated with Tourettes syndrome; uncontrollable head and shoulder jerking, body jerking, and arm flailing movements. At times these were constant, up to 300 or more a day. I also had other neurological disorders associated with Tourettes syndrome; which were depression, increased irritability, aggression, increased sensory desensitivity, impaired social skills, and concentration problems.

Since October of 1997, when my Tourettes syndrome worsened, I have had increased problems with handling the stress of working as a Registered Nurse in a busy hospital; thereby making the symptoms worse and have been in and out of work on disability. I've been on disability for a total of 14 months and have been placed on various medications to control the symptoms of Tourettes syndrome. None of them worked and many had very serious side effects the result was that I was unable to function and had to stay with my parents.

I have always had a strong faith in God and the Catholic Church. I believed that He would heal me so I started going to healing services. I also had Christian friends pray over me and became involved in a Bible Study group. Prayer and reading the Word of God daily has greatly increased my faith and I believed that God was going to heal me of the Tourettes syndrome.

I prayed the scriptures and faith vision daily for months, truly believing that God was healing me of the Tourettes and thanked him for doing so. Last month, October of 1998, I went to the healing mass at St. Pius X Roman Catholic Church. I was prayed over and "rested in the Spirit". I believed that God had healed me. Since that night the violent tics, tremors, sensitivity to noise, and other problems that I had associated with Tourettes syndrome have gone away. I'm on a very small, almost non-therapeutic, dose of a medication that never worked before. I also have none of the horrible side effects that I used to get from high doses of the medication! I've been cleared to go back to work. The hospital is looking for a position for me, since they filled my old position while I was on disability. I thank God every morning and night for this healing and continue to pray, go to mass more often during the week, and read the Bible. There is power in prayer and in the word of God! All you need is faith.

186

A.B.

I am thankful and thank God every day for my healing. On February 28th I went to the hospital with a temperature and sores in my mouth. I also had swollen glands. The doctor came into see me and admitted me for two days.

March 1- Blood test and a CAT scan of the throat and neck were taken. The doctor discovered a mass behind my thyroid. I went home from the hospital.

March 5th- 6th- The doctor ordered a thyroid scan. The mass was still present. The doctor sent me to a specialist.

March 17th- Another sonogram.

March 29th- Buffalo Ultra Sound for another scan.

I attended the healing mass at St. Pius X Church on March 23 or March 27th. On April 8, I went to the hospital and had an Echo Exam of the neck, head, and a biopsy of the mass.

On June 23rd, I went for another CAT scan and the doctors could not find the mass.

Another doctor was called and he said all they could find was an artifact. On August 17, I went to my doctor and he said that the mass was gone. He said that he knew what he saw, but I have no sign of the mass now. He asked if I'd been to a healing mass. I replied that yes, I'd been to a healing mass, and had prayers prayed over me.

Between February 28 and August 17th I had seen two doctors and my personal doctor many many times.

Thank God I'm cured. No trace of anything.

R.G.

In July 1998, I became ill and underwent extensive surgery. The cause of my surgery was colon cancer.

Of course, cancer is a deadly word. The first thing that entered my mind was how much time do I have? I didn't want to know, neither did I want to put any more stress on my husband and children.

I turned to our Lord and asked him to help me get through this. I started my chemo two months later praying through all my sessions. My husband and I have always been devoted Catholics; we started coming to St. Pius X and St. Margaret's healing masses. We made visits to Father Baker's Basilica with all my love and prayers to Jesus and the Holy Spirit. I asked Jesus to help me get my health and strength back. After one year of chemo my doctor sent me to Kenmore Mercy Hospital and St. Joseph's Hospital to undergo more tests. The day I received a clean bill of health was one of the happiest days of my life. I still go for blood work and check ups. I can't thank God enough for answering all my prayers.

I know I can't see Jesus but I know he is near me and hears my every prayer.

Don't ever stop praying and always keep the faith. He helped me and He will help you too.

God Bless Everyone

S.K.

I am here to give witness to the great healing I have experienced. I heard about these healing masses right after being diagnosed with cancer. My husband and I were visiting some very special friends on a Sunday and we asked if they knew of a church that had evening mass. They said they thought that St. Pius X Church did. We called St. Pius and they said no, but stated that the next evening they were offering a healing mass. My husband and I decided to attend the healing mass and we have been attending ever since. We know God works in mysterious ways, finding this service was certainly His doing. One evening attending a healing mass at St. Margaret's, I experienced something that I hope everyone will have the opportunity to experience. When Tony laid his hands on me I rested in the Spirit and saw this bright light. I knew then that I was cancer free. I felt a peace that can't be explained unless you experience it yourself. The best way to explain it, is that it is like having a baby. You don't know what it's like until you experience it yourself. I have had two major surgeries since then and all the biopsies came back clear. I truly believe things happen for a reason and my experience with cancer has changed my whole life (especially my relationship with God.)

Murphy Bova

5/18/99

I am self-employed as a Tax Accountant. On January 8, of this year, I had my eyes checked up and my doctor told me that I should have surgery, to remove a cataract in my left eye. I replied "No way, I can't, I have a heavy tax schedule from January 15 to April 20, 1999. Not only that, my wife is going for hip surgery in June of this year." The doctor suggested that I make another appointment for April 30, 1999, after tax season.

I kept my April 30 eye appointment. The eye doctor examined my eyes and said, "Your eye looks good, very healthy for your age. No operation this year, let's make another appointment for the year 2000 in May."

When I got home and told my wife, she was relieved and surprised. My son said, "It's a miracle! Remember the healing mass at St. Margaret's Church when Tony Cubello prayed over you, on February 8? Could it be?" "Yes!" I shouted, "the healing mass." The Holy Spirit had answered our prayers.

Diana C. Augustine

Here is a letter of thanksgiving for healing received this year.

I survived breast cancer in 1992. In June, I was diagnosed with a large cyst on my left ovary with a small nodule next to it. This was very dangerous since I was post menopausal, over 60, and had a history of breast cancer. My gynecologist recommended immediate surgery. I refused because I was spending the summer out west with my grandchildren.

My doctor was very upset with my decision, continuing to insist that I needed surgery NOW. I told her that nothing was going to interfere with my plans and to schedule surgery for the fall and to write "patient uncooperative", if she needed to document anything. She reluctantly agreed to delay my operation.

My husband and I have attended several healing masses in the area and were especially drawn to the beauty of the service at St. Pius X Church. As soon as we enter the church we feel surrounded by God, His Holy Spirit, His angels and Saints, and especially by His Blessed Mother. Since childhood I have had a strong devotion to Mary.

After diagnosis, I called the healing ministry to pray for me, as well as for my husband and my brother, who were also having health problems. During the summer I continued to pray for healing and for the strength and courage to deal with whatever God allowed into my life. I asked Mother Mary to help me as I walked the mountain trails, played with my grandchildren, lit candles at our home and in church. I never doubted that my healing would occur even when the pain in my pelvic area increased.

In September, following my husband's successful surgery, I had my left ovary removed. Everyone who had contact with me from pre-operation to discharge treated me with kindness, no matter how busy or tired they were. I remember lying on the operating table asking the Blessed Mother to hold my hand and to guide the doctors during my surgery. I recovered quickly with absolutely no pain or discomfort. I had no need for the strong painkillers that were prescribed, not even for Tylenol! Two days later, on my birthday, the doctor's office informed me officially there were no malignancies. My prayers were answered. Also, my brother's condition has stabilized and my husband and I continue to enjoy health and an active lifestyle.

Thank you, Lord Jesus, for these healings. Thank you Mother Mary for your intercession. Thank you Queen of Peace Healing Ministry. I felt the power of your prayers. Thank you for doing God's work.

Pamela Gaglione

December 16, 2002

I hereby give witness to God's healing in my life. Back in April of 2001, I ran across a quote and thought it was good, and I jotted it down. Little did I know that approximately one month later that quote would have such a powerful impact on my life. The quote was "IF GOD'S HAND IS IN ALL THINGS, THEN LEAVE ALL THINGS IN GOD'S HANDS!!!!" It was a message of FAITH!!!!

In May of 2001, I had been experiencing hearing loss for approximately six months. Not much was made of it until I found a new doctor who took it more seriously. It was then that I was diagnosed with an extremely rare brain/skull based tumor. Approximately 23 known cases of this type of tumor have ever existed in the world. The tumor did massive destruction. It destroyed a good portion of my temporal skull; it destroyed the bones of my left ear, it destroyed my TMJ joint; it was all over my facial nerve and it was all over my ceratoid artery.

The doctors told me that this type of surgery is one of the most intricate, dangerous surgeries of all, because the skull base is such a very delicate, intricate area to perform surgery on. In fact, surgery would not have even been an option for me fifteen years ago. I had three surgeons on my case. They each gave me the realistic possible outcomes of the surgery, which initially, horrified me. I was informed that the TMJ joint would have to be totally removed which would cause my face to be disfigured. I pleaded with the doctor and asked if something else could be done. He told me the main reason for this surgery was to remove the tumor and that it was going to be a very long surgery, and that maybe at another time they could go back in and reconstruct it. He said that I might be looking at several surgeries down the road. Because the tumor was all over the facial nerve, I may have either permanent or temporary facial paralysis; affecting both my eyes and mouth region, the cochlear in my ear region would have to removed, leaving me with hearing problems, balance and vestibule problems in addition to ongoing nausea.

After hearing this, I was very scared. I asked God, why me? Then I realized that if I asked why me, then I would also have to ask him why he had given me so many blessings in my life.

To be very honest with you, I cried about three times initially. I did not want to die. But, something very powerful overcame me, which I believe to be the grace of the Holy Spirit and at that point I thought, "How can I lose? I am in a win-win situation! If I live I get to be with my friends and loved ones. If I die, I will get to be with God in heaven. How can I lose? And I began to trust, and put it at the foot of the cross, and into God's hands. I believe very strongly that God was going to heal me, if it was His Will.

Not my will, but His. And I knew that if I was not healed, that I would still be in God's hands and that he would be with me always and see me through everything!

About thirteen years ago, I began to attend healing masses given by Father Matthew Swizdor. We attended for my sister who had been diagnosed with an advanced case of Hodgkin's disease. My sister did receive a healing and in fact gave her testimony here last summer. When I was diagnosed, I decided to attend a healing mass given by the Queen of Peace Healing Ministry here at St. Pius X Church. I remember at the beginning of the service that Tony told us that they would be praying for all types of healings that night and then went on to name a few specific healings. When he mentioned brain tumors, I thought Oh, someone must have told Tony that I was coming tonight. No one had told Tony! It was divine intervention.

A week before my surgery, the Queen of Peace Healing Ministry had come to my home for private prayer. When Tony laid his hands on my head, I felt the most incredible sense of the Peace of Christ that I had never felt before. And what was so amazing is that others in the room had also felt this peace. Tony also prayed that I would not have pain through all of the surgery and after.

The doctor told me that I was facing a sixteen to eighteen hour operation, but the night before the surgery, I slept soundly and peacefully.

When I went in for the surgery, I knew that Jesus was right there with me, holding me throughout the surgery and guiding the surgeon's hands. The surgery was very successful. They were able to perform the operation in twelve hours instead of the sixteen to eighteen hours. They placed a titanium plate in my skull to replace the damage done by the tumor. They were able to remove the tumor without touching the facial nerve. They were able to leave the cochlear in. They were able to remove the tumor that was all over my carotid artery. And amazingly, they were able to leave half of my TMJ joint in place and reconstruct the other half. I have no facial paralysis or facial deformity at all. I had no pain throughout my surgery or after. In fact, I never used the pain medication that they sent home with me. I went home in six days, and about four days later my doctor told me to go out and live my life!

Initially, he had told me that I was going to be plagued with this problem for the rest of my life. That was not the case now. I went through 28 days of radiation to prevent reoccurrence with minimal side effects. I do have hearing loss in my left ear because of the damage. It has been a year and a half since my surgery with no reoccurrence of the tumor. My doctors and medical personnel marvel at my recovery. My primary doctor told me that I was a living miracle!

I was and still am very blessed by God to have an incredibly, loving support system in my family, friends and others that were praying for me. I am very blessed to have had the support and prayers of the Queen of Peace Healing Ministry and to have the opportunity to attend the healing masses at St. Pius X and to have the ministry come to my home.

It is important for me to say that I not only received a

physical healing, but I also believe that I received a spiritual healing as well. I believe that faith always brings us through tough times and trials and that God will always sustain us and see us through whatever our problems may be. Although I have always been a believer in Jesus, my relationship with God has never been stronger. God is the focal point of my life. I strongly believe in the power of prayer, and I try every day to live a life of prayer.

When I tell people of my healing, many are amazed and say to me that God must have a purpose for my life. I believe that God has a purpose for all of us and that we are here to love and serve God in every way that we can.

No matter what we may be going through, I believe that God will always turn it around and use it for something good! It's about faith and it's about trusting God. I would like to end with scripture from James Chapter 1:

"Consider it pure joy my brothers, whenever you face trials of many kinds, because you know that the testing of your faith develops perseverance. Perseverance must finish its work so that you may be mature and complete, not lacking anything." (James 1:2-4)

Thank you. God Bless all of you!

Linda Smalter

3/24/03

Five and one-half years ago, my mother was diagnosed with lung cancer. I took her to the healing mass at St. Pius X Church. The healing service was conducted by the Queen of Peace Healing Ministry. She went up to the altar for the laying on of hands and when Tony laid hands on her she rested in the Spirit. After the service and on the way home, she asked "Do you smell the roses?" She was referring to an experience known as the "odor of holiness" and a sign of the Virgin Mary being present. She smelled the aroma for days afterwards. She had surgery for her lung cancer. Surgery went fine! Praise the Lord!

However, we were not prepared for the very hard recovery. She was not able to breathe on her own and could not come off the respirator. Days were passing and I called the Queen of Peace Healing Ministry. They came to her bedside in ICU. The ministry prayed over her with the laying on of hands. It was a very beautiful sight to see the Holy Spirit's love flowing over my mother in the ICU Room at Roswell Hospital. The next day she was up and sitting in a chair and off the respirator! Praise God, she was healed by the power of the Holy Spirit and God's undying love. To this day there is no return of cancer.

My second story is about My Uncle Bob and his fiancée Paula. Paula came to St. Pius X Church in December 2002. We came for the healing mass of the Queen of Peace Healing Ministry. She stood in as proxy for her sister, who was scheduled for surgery. Paula went up for the laying on of hands. She rested in the Spirit for quite awhile. On the way home she acted quite different. I asked her if she was OK. She replied, "Did you see what I saw?" She said "I saw the face of Jesus and the Virgin Mary". Paula's sister went for an ultrasound. The tumor was gone. Praise God from whom all blessings flow! She was healed by his Grace and Love.

We had a mini healing service at our house with the Queen of Peace Healing Ministry. Uncle Bob stood in as proxy for Paula. Tony laid hands on Uncle Bob. His throat became red hot. You could see it across the room. It turned out that Paula had throat problems and she was healed. All Glory and Honor to Our Lord. He healed her throat.

My last story is about a dear friend Mary. Mary was diagnosed with a rare type of cancer. Even the Cleveland Clinic could not help her. She was sent to Bethesda, Maryland to the National Institute of Health. She had to prepare six weeks before the scheduled surgery.

I brought Mary to the healing mass at St. Pius X Church with the Queen of Peace Healing Ministry. Tony laid hands on her. She said she felt peace. She also came to our house for a healing service with the Queen of Peace Healing Ministry. I had several people there that evening. I didn't even know them all, but the Holy Spirit guided them to our house. My dear husband, Steve, and I were more than happy to make everyone feel welcome. Many people rested in the Spirit that night in our living room. Mary had her surgery. She is now home and healing, as the surgery was a success with the removal of several tumors. She is resting as the Holy Spirit lets His love flow over her and heals her body, mind, and soul. Thanks be to God.

Thanks to the Queen of Peace Healing Ministry. They have helped so many people.

S.P.G.

In September of 1998 I was diagnosed as having a lump in my right breast. My doctor sent me for a mammogram to confirm this, and the radiologist said it was a fibroid cyst.

The radiologist advised me to stay away from caffeine and to come back for a follow-up exam in 6 months. I was nervous and upset about this because they were not 100% positive about what type of cyst this was. Shortly after, I attended a Healing Mass at St. Pius X and was prayed over by Tony Cubello. I again went to the doctor for a follow-up visit and was told that the cyst had become larger. The doctor explained that when I next returned for my 6 month check up, if the cyst became even larger I would have to have it aspirated by a needle.

Again, I went to another healing mass at St. Pius X and once again was prayed over. This time I experienced a feeling coming over me that made me feel that something was different. I knew in my heart, that I was being healed. I was no longer afraid to go back to the doctor for my next follow-up. When I went to my next appointment, the doctor did another mammogram and the doctor called me into his office to look over the x-ray. We were astonished, the doctor said the cyst was completely gone. He shook his head and could not believe it.

I told him I had gone to several healing masses and he said although he could not explain it, "if it works, just keep on going!!!" The Lord is present where two or more are gathered and He does work through the prayers of His People. I give testimony to that this day.

196

M.A.

I was given the opportunity to testify to our Lord's healing power at the February 28, 2000 healing mass at St. Pius X.

It was Monday evening, January 31, 2000 at St. Pius X Church, the monthly healing Mass. My sister had been coming here for several years; when her son, Jim was diagnosed with his illness in 1998, I began joining my sister, mainly to give her support. But I soon found it to be a place of peace and healing for myself as well. My sister and I always felt a real peace at these masses and the peace went home with us. The day before, my nephew had consented to a priest visiting him at his home and he was finally able to be reconciled and to find peace. Perhaps it was this miracle that assured us God was answering our prayers, but that night in particular, I sensed a deep peace flow throughout me.

The next evening, I learned that my nephew had been taken to the hospital where he went into a coma. The next morning he went home to our Father in heaven. As I reflected on all that happened during theses final months, I realized and believe that Jim was given the spiritual healing he so desperately needed. Yes, he was not able to come to seek healing himself, but the faith and prayers of his mom, family and friends stormed the heavens with prayers. We all would have wanted Jim to be physically healed, but our God knew he needed spiritual healing. There is no more pain or suffering to endure. He is at peace with our Lord and with all his family who were waiting for him to join them. I firmly believe that he is with us in a deeper more spiritual way than ever before.

I would like to thank St. Pius and their healing ministry. You are truly a gift from God.

May the Lord bless and guide you in your wonderful work.

D.K.

10-11-97

I am here today to give witness and thank God for the "little things" or graces in my life. My healing is not of great proportions. I haven't experienced a religious conversion or a miracle physical healing. My healing is one of great awareness of the "little things"

In January of this past year you could say I was a bit depressed. I was unable to cope with my family or myself. I had no patience with my children. (two toddlers and a baby). I was always yelling or screaming at them. Most days I just couldn't wait for my husband to get home. But when he got home I usually greeted him with some sort of attitude he didn't deserve. I'm not sure why they put up with me but they did. On top of that, I hated the way I looked and none of my clothes fit. I always felt frumpy.

I tried to talk to a few friends but it always sounded unjustified. When you live in a big house, stay home to take care of your three healthy daughters and your husband works hard and comes home to be a great father and supportive husband; it really isn't justified. But this didn't change the way I felt. I began to pray the rosary but I seldom prayed the whole rosary or often enough.

In February, a friend told me of her experience at this healing mass at St. Pius X Church and how she rested in the Spirit. So I attended at the end of the month, while there, I was overcome by the Holy Spirit and felt that I wasn't worthy of God's love and forgiveness.

In March, I had dinner with a bunch of friends. One of whom told me how important it is to pray the rosary everyday. So I started that night and I haven't missed a day since. Once in a while it is only a partial rosary. I pray for patience and understanding.

In April, I got this overwhelming desire to go back to confession. I hadn't been to confession since I was maybe 10 years old. Well I went twice in April to make sure I confessed everything and was forgiven.

Since then I have noticed "little things". I'm able to enjoy my children even during temper tantrums. I'm able to stop, pray, and then talk reasonably with my husband, when I would rather have an attitude. "Seek and you shall find, ask and you will receive." I have a true understanding of the bible verse. I would like to thank this ministry for saying "yes" to God's will, for without them I may not have grown this much. This was the first time I gave my will to God.

B.P.

10/17/00

I reside in the Town of Wheatfield. I'm here tonight to tell how I began coming to St. Pius X, and my experiences from the healing masses.

I have been coming to St. Pius X for about a year and a half. It all began on February 10, 1999. I was diagnosed with metastasized breast cancer which means it already spread to my lungs, bones, spine, with tumors in my neck, under the left arm and in the humerus bone. I was told I could not be cured, but my life could be prolonged, for how long, we did not know. There would be no surgery because of how this disease had already spread. Chemotherapy and possibly radiation was the suggested treatment. The worst thing that I recall on that day after the initial shock, was how to tell my children, especially my daughter whose wedding date was already arranged.

After that day was over, all the tests began. During one of these tests, there is a two hour waiting process and you are allowed to leave. My friend asked what I would like to do, and I replied, "you know that church we keep passing? I would like to make a visit there." That church was St. Pius X. I prayed for courage and strength.

Treatment began in March 1999, and I didn't think of St. Pius X again until one day in May when a friend approached me telling me of a healing mass. By that time, I had attended several healing masses thinking that this might be one of the same. This friend told me that date and time and asked if I knew where St. Pius X Church was. I replied that I knew exactly where it is and believed the Lord had started to answer my prayers by leading me back to St. Pius X.

I attended my first healing mass in May with my husband and was overwhelmed. I did not know what to expect, felt a little afraid, but was put at ease by people sitting next to me. After the laying on of hands by Tony, there was no instant miracle, but I felt different. It's hard to explain, but coping with the treatments seemed less difficult and I continued to lead as close to a normal life as possible. I continued to attend the healing masses, hoping my miracle would be seeing my daughter married.

I finished 9 months of chemo and was told this disease could start up again elsewhere at any time. Things had already started to change, but I did not realize it. I was told I didn't have to receive medication intravenously monthly for my bones because my bones were healing by themselves.

At one of the healing masses and after the laying on of hands by Tony, I rested in the Spirit and felt a tightness go across my chest. I did not know what this meant until a few months later when I had a chest x-ray. The x-ray revealed my lungs were clear. There were to be no more tests till after my daughter's wedding.

The time did arrive and my husband and I witnessed our daughter's wedding. It was cold and rainy that day, but as my daughter said " It was the most beautiful day in her life as both her parents were there to share it with her." My prayers were answered and I believed this to be my miracle.

The time approached when I had to be re-tested. The x-rays and scans were scheduled in the beginning of July. My doctor informed me that the sonogram of the liver showed what could be some metastic deposits and also gave me the written report, so I could read this for myself. These deposits did not show on previous scans. It was advised to have another CAT scan of the liver. This was scheduled for July 26th. My family and I were very distraught over the news. There was a healing mass scheduled on July 24th which I attended with a friend hoping to find strength and courage to face this test. Before the laying on of hands, Tony said, "I'm praying tonight for someone with various forms of cancer and a problem with the liver. We were both in awe. I went up for the laying on of hands that night and did not feel as afraid anymore. On Wednesday, July 26th, I had the CAT scan done and was very calm during the procedure. On the next visit to the doctor in August, I was told my liver was clear and my bones were stabilizing. The lump under my left arm is just about gone.

I don't know if I'll ever be completely cured or what God has in store for me, but I will continue to attend the healing masses and as I attend each one, I thank God because he has given me four more weeks of life. My family and I are closer than ever because of this disease and realize what is important in life. My husband lost his first wife to cancer and has fought twice as hard for me with all his loving words of encouragement. I even renewed an old friendship and she now comes with me to the healing masses monthly.

Some miracles do not happen spontaneously as I thought, but if you have faith, God does listen, cares and will help you in His way and His time, whether it might be in a day or a year. I wanted to tell of my experiences as my thanks to God and possibly touch someone out there that is afraid as I was. Thank you to all that help out in any way with these healing masses and God Bless.

L.S.

10/18/97

This letter is in regard to the healing received by 3 small children in my family. At. ages of 2, 4 and 5 years these 3 children were sexually abused and raped by someone who was trusted. The children were threatened and told not to tell or their mother would be hurt. We are not totally sure what other kinds of threats were made to keep them quiet.

Finally, it was found out and the children were immediately moved to a safe and secure location. The effects of these events were that the children had behavioral and sleep problems. They were very afraid of people, especially men.

We started bringing the children to the healing masses and prayed continuously for them. The biggest effect seems to be the healing of memories. After all of this came out, the children talked about it quite a bit. It hasn't been mentioned in a few months now, and the older 2 children are sleeping really well. The youngest child still has some difficulty sleeping, which we know will fade as the healing continues.

The children's behavior has improved and they are learning to trust again. One child, who rested in the spirit for at least 15 minutes, has really been remarkable. After this beautiful experience he, at 5 years of age, said 15 decades of the rosary with his grandmother and aunt in one day.

The oldest 2 are doing well in school and the youngest is looking forward to her new experience of day care, and being with other children.

My family and I would like to thank the healing ministry and also the Pastor at St. Pius X. for the children's protection.

Maureen T. Schmitt

5/16/03

God works in mysterious ways! Throughout my husband Peter's seven year battle with cancer our faith that God was guiding us grew day by day. His initial prognosis was somewhat grim, but through positive attitude and constant treatment, doors seemed to keep opening for us and little rays of hope had always shown through. Every time we would hit a valley God would strengthen us to carry on. We traveled near and far for medical treatments and left no stone unturned.

As it became clearer to us that God was calling Peter home, a friend suggested that we invite the Queen of Peace Healing Ministry into our home to pray for healing, along with some of our family members and close friends. Tony Cubello prayed for and with Peter for his healing and the strength to accept God's wishes. The gift all of us received that evening was ever so powerful. The ministry's love and faith surrounded us. As we recited the Rosary together, Peter was gaining peace within his heart. God was putting all the pieces in place.

Three days later, our parish priest stopped in because he was driving by our house, passed it, and turned around because of an inner calling he heard. He and Peter talked for awhile followed by the Sacraments of Reconciliation and the Holy Eucharist. Two days after that, a friend we hadn't seen in over a year who is an Extraordinary Minister visited unannounced, because he thought of Peter that morning in church and brought the Eucharist. Although Peter passed away the next day, he was truly filled with the Holy Spirit, surrounded by people that loved him and ready to accept God's wishes.

How do I ever thank your ministry enough for the love you showed us during Peter's last days? You not only gave Peter peace in his heart, but also peace to our entire family. God works in beautiful and mysterious ways and all of you are truly messengers of the Lord. God Bless.

THE "COACH"

Mike Fennell was more than the above title. He was an outstanding athlete, friend to many, loving husband and father, but most of all, a man of faith and courage. Fennell, 42, had non-smoker's lung cancer. I first met Mike Fennell when I was asked to pray over him at the residence of a member of my ministry. He came in from Rochester, New York with his wife Erin and his sister, Pam Baker. There were three ministry people also present.

As I laid hands on Mike and prayed, he came under the power of God's Holy Spirit. When Mike came out of this state of ecstasy, he said that he felt heat, a tingling sensation and deep peace. Next, we prayed for Mike's wife, Erin. She experienced peace with the vision of Jesus and Mary walking on either side of Mike and smiling. As I prayed over Erin, Mike who was across the room kneeling in prayer, was again overcome by the power of God and began to move his head from side to side. He later told us that Jesus held his head in his hands, rocking it from side to side and told us that Jesus said, "Tell them that I am here". Lastly, we prayed for Mike's sister Pam; who through much peace and tears, received a conversion in the form of a deeper relationship with Jesus and an insight to priority values in her life.

Mike Fennell's baseball skills had often put him in the spotlight. An outstanding catcher at Fairport High School, then a first-team NCAA all-American catcher at Le Moyne College, he was later drafted by the New York Yankees. He spent three years as a bullpen catcher for the Yankees. Through the years, he contributed to winning seasons and several titles. He was once a teammate of John Elway, when the former NFL star was playing baseball in the Yankees farm system. Mike was in his ninth year as varsity coach at McQuaid Jesuit High School in Rochester, New York.

Mike's words to describe his loss of hair due to his treatments of chemo and radiation: "just think of all the money I've saved on haircuts". His team at McQuaid shaved their heads to support him through chemotherapy. On their hats they inscribed his number, 55. "Coaching gives me something to look forward to", Fennell said.

"He had faith," says his wife. "He wanted to make sure he won this battle." A battle his three children also wanted to see him win. His son Ryan, 11, says his goal is to play baseball for his dad at McQuaid. His daughters, Kaelen, 8, and Meghan, 5, had spent many spring and summer afternoons at the baseball diamond, playing or watching games with their father. Fennell planned to continue coaching his three children who play baseball or softball.

Since his initial diagnosis in 2000, Mike had shown remarkable courage and determination. He had seemingly endless treatments of chemotherapy and radiation. His positive attitude to beat the toughest opponent of his life had made him a role model for cancer patients throughout the area. The Wilmot Cancer Center honored Fennell with the 2002 Inspiration Award; former recipients of this award include: figure skater Scott Hamilton and Army General Norman Schwarzkopf.

The 42 year-old Rochester resident had always relied on his faith in God for strength; this had been especially true when his treatments were difficult. Shortly after his diagnosis, he traveled to Medjugorje, a spiritual haven where people claim to have seen the Virgin Mary and where several healings have been reported. "Mike's fight against cancer has touched so many people in so many different ways," says Erin, Mike's wife. "We are so thankful for the number of well wishes and prayers we receive. They are much appreciated throughout our whole family. We believe strongly in the power of prayer."

The "Coach" has since passed on to be with his God, but through all his trials many hearts have been touched and brought closer to He who created us all. Mike left us with his priorities in order:

His Love for God
His Love for Family
His Love for the game of baseball

As Mike departed from the church at his funeral mass, we heard the lone trumpeter bidding goodbye to "The Coach" to the tune of: "Take Me Out to the Ball Game".

Michael John Fennell

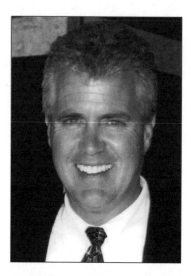

MORE WORDS FROM HEAVEN

(464) 2/24/93

Again, I say I will bless you in ministry, even though it seems not so, at this time. More events will take place, manifesting My signs to you that I am working in your life. Have I not said to watch for the little signs so that you will know they are of Me?

(465-466) 2/24/93

This world seems to beg for punishment as few succumb to My teachings, My Commandments. There is no love for neighbor. The earth is steeped in pride and greed. None or hardly any come to visit Me in My exposed presence on the altar. My Heart bled for them, but most shed not a tear for Me. Come, My son, often, to keep company with Me, to speak with Me and let us pray for those so distant from My Sacred Heart. Moreover, organize with those of prayer. Assist in "true" evangelization, and pray over My people for ongoing conversion of the heart. Be among My apostles of these latter days and always join My priest son, in any way, to lead others to Me. I come in this Holy Season as the Prince of Peace. Spread peace wherever you go. Be a peacemaker and the Kingdom of God will be yours. I have chosen you as a son of the Most High. Pray always in the Name of the Father, and of the Son and of the Holy Spirit and My peace will follow you.

(468) 2/25/93

My Mother and I both know of your plight. Take faith as your weapon and confront the enemy, knowing that through this faith, your belief in My Words and the messages of My Mother will come to pass. Be stout-hearted, My warrior son, and let My grace come down upon you, to strengthen your belief and your perseverance. I have sustained you, thus far, and I will continue to sustain you. You will be freed to service Me, as I have chosen this path for you. You will be what I have molded you to be: a member of the "army of My Mother."

(471) 3/4/93

I have called you into service ...

(472) 3/6/93

...to be a conductor of My power. Soon you will service Me, according to My instructions. You will lay hands upon the sick and they will recover. But, mostly, they will be converted to Me, through you, by the imposition of your hands, of which represent My grace upon them. You will become what I want you to be: a servant of these last times. Always pray, always fast, always call upon My name as you lay hands in the Name of the Father, and of the Son and of the Holy Spirit.

(473) 3/7/93

Our Lady

You will be persecuted, misled and ridiculed, but you will survive all because you speak in the name of my Son.

(474) 3/11/93

Be vigilante in the ways of the Spirit. I will give you discernment to further your ministry. Be patient and know that you will be used in a powerful way at the time I choose.

(477) 3/20/93

Listen to the words of the holy priest, then spread this message to others for he speaks the truth and is united to My scriptural words.

It is necessary that all follow My Commandments, especially in these, the last days.

(478) 3/21/93

Be considerate of those who do not know Me. Introduce them to Me in a kind, gentle manner. Let them know of eternal life, of what is beyond the life of this earth. Let them know that to be with Me is to be bliss, forever.

(479-480) 3/24/93

Persist as I lead you to more ministry. Ask My priest son to assist for many will come to conversion through you. Soon more manifestations will occur and more salvation will begin among My people. You will be instrumental in these works. That is why your persecution is at hand. Leave the earthly problems to Me. Look only to your spiritual life and I will solve all. I will open the hearts of priests to allow you to lay your hands upon My people. Have I not said that My other sons would lead you to this? You are chosen and those of whom I choose will participate in the works of the Kingdom. Be consistent in your prayer and fasting so that the evil one cannot get a hold on you.

(482) 3/26/93

Offer up all your sufferings to Me and you will live eternal life with Me, My Mother and the Court of Heaven.

(483) 3/28/93

I will commence to allow certain events to take place in your life as to enhance your spiritual understanding of the ministry of which I said would be like no other.

(484) 3/30/93

If you want answers, My son, pray to My Mother and She will answer you. She is your prayer partner. No one is closer to you than She.

(490) 4/3/93

Come closer to Me, My son, let My words permeate your being.

Be always on the alert for the enemy lurks to secure My people in the moments of weakness. Be vigilant and conduct yourself in a manner befitting Christian propriety.

(491) 4/4/93

Listen to the least of My children, as they approach you, soon.

Let them pour out their hearts to you. Then, pray over them so that I can minister to them, through you. Have I not said that you will be My instrument of love and compassion as you pray in My Name?

(497-498) 4/11/93

All the people of this world will be shaken with fear as time goes on. There will be chaos as the new sufferings come upon them. They will not be prepared as they have no awareness of life hereafter. They live only for the moment. Gather My remnant, plan means of converting any of My little ones that may be saved, for the time of chastisement grows near. I will begin to show you where you are to minister. Be alert, be prepared, be in a state of grace to impose your hands, to pray and allow Me to work in their lives. Read the messages, to encourage them and the others who do not know Me, witness, for I will give you the words. Ask for more witness from the others. Testimonies, from those who believe, enhances the faith of the unbelievers that are present, even those with weak faith are touched. This is what I taught, this is what I preached, this is what you are to do. Urge your sisters and brothers to witness, also, and see the fruits pour forth. Make this a part of your prayer gatherings, for it is directed to uplift the spirits of My brethren and will ultimately result in glory to Me. We must pray with My people. This is a positive accomplishment if you are to heed the words I give to you.

(502) 4/15/93

You have had a bad day, have you not? Offer all up to Me for the release of souls from purgatory. I have a purpose for all that I do.

Rejoice and know that through the pain, the persecution and the tears, I will bring peace and holiness to you. I am the light of the world and I will shine down on you and cover you with My light of Divine Mercy.

(505) 4/18/93

Your efforts will not go unnoticed as you have prevailed of yourself in your endeavors to assist My people, in many ways. I will continue to bless you as you continue to minister. The fruits will become apparent and My Spirit will be known to those who begin to follow Me.

(506) 4/18/93

I will be with you in prayer as you pray with the flock. Pray for Wisdom and Knowledge. Fast on that day, and the fruits, the special graces, will be given as you lay your hands upon them. Believe and they will be converted and healed. Go in the peace of your Lord and your Heavenly Mother.

(507) 4/18/93

I am the light of the world. He who believes in Me, shall never die.

I died so that you may live. Now, you are to live for Me, through Me and are to follow all of My Commandments. This teaching is for the benefit of My children, everywhere! My Mercy will prevail if My words are heeded, but for the deaf of spirit, they will not see the Light of Heaven.

(508) 4/22/93

This is a time for prayer. My heart longs for My little ones to come to Me in My presence in the Blessed Sacrament. There, all will find Me. There, all will find peace. There, the weak will become strong and there, they will also find My Mother, the Mother of all My children.

(512) 4/24/93

Our Lady

The words I give today are words of sorrow. My Immaculate Heart pines for those of my children who will be lost forever. I ask for increased prayers for this is a time of urgency. The cup has overflowed.

(513) 4/25/93

Our Lady

Be prepared to do battle as the spiritual war of these times begins.

My remnant army will be gathered and immersed in my Immaculate Heart. The time of testing is upon us. There will be pleas for mercy as the sufferings commence. Those who are covered by the Precious Blood of my Son and those who remain under my Mantle shall not fear. Be at peace and know that our protection will be yours.

(514-515) 4/28/93

Our Lady

Because of your persistence, the fruits will emerge. Call upon the Name of my Son, Jesus. Call upon His Holy Spirit for revelations of what He wants done, this night. The power will be present and this ministry will begin in full blossom, as the time of year of full blossom.

Let nothing dissuade your perseverance, but continue on as has been directed by my Son. A continuous number of healing prayers will be forthcoming as you battle for souls in the name of the "Prince of Peace". Let your concern at this time be regarding prayer for my little ones, as time is not in abundance. I will lead you in any areas of which you have doubts. The answers will be given you as you proceed in this direction. You will obtain power from above so that the Will of my Son will be fulfilled. Leave all details to us, stay in an attitude of prayer, listen and hear us as We speak to your spirit.

(536) 5/20/93

You will be blessed by My Holy Spirit. All will come

to fruition, as I have told you. I have prepared you
for this ministry and the gates of hell will not prevail
against My wishes. You will be fortified by My love
and My power and, as always, My Mother prays
with you. My blood covers you. The mantle of My
Mother covers you. Be at peace, for you represent
Me.

(540) 5/22/93

He is trying to get to you, is he not? Do not let him
succeed, as he harasses those who try to live My precepts. My power is such that you may use it to ward
off the evil one; however, that is where your faith
level will surface. Rebuke him, every time, in My
Name and you will persevere in order to accomplish
My works as you have been called to, in the ministry
of love and compassion for My glory and for My
people. Be at peace, in My love!

(547) 5/30/93

Come deeper into My Heart, My son. Learn more of
the truths of why I died for you and the others. You
have had but a taste of the persecution meted out to
Me by those whom I loved and nurtured. Turn all
your compassion to My people and be at their disposal, as they need your prayers.

(548) 5/31/93

Do just what I have led you to do, in your thoughts.
These are My thoughts implanted in your mind and
in your heart. You will travel in ministry!

(550) 5/31/93

Be pleased My little son, that I have chosen you to

carry on these works through My Holy Spirit. I do not select My chosen children because of worldly talents or their positions in life, but rather I choose those whom I know will carry out My desires to enhance My Kingdom by leading souls to Me through the ministries which I select for them.

(551) 5/31/93

Our Lady

More manifestation will prevail as I come to you in the ministry, given to you by my Son. The people will increase and your words will increase. All will come to you as you pray and listen to Our direction.

Ask for testimony at the proper moments. Do not force issues, but be at peace in all that you do. My mantle covers you as you lay your hands upon those who come before you. More and unusual events will ensue as you follow the path that my Son has designed for you. Take one day at a time, and invoke the Holy Spirit of my Son, whenever you pray and impose your hands. Your peace will not be shaken, as I pray with you, my little son.

(558-560) 6/11/93

All the distractions of the day will slowly fade away and you will again know that it is I, your Savior, who remains with you in the lonely hours. I comfort you, as does My Holy Mother. You will soon experience much joy in the days to come. Be aware that the enemy lurks near, at all times, wherever My Mother is venerated. Countless souls need nourishment of the Spirit. Be My representative of love and compassion. As I said to Peter:

Feed My lambs.

Feed My sheep.

I say now these same words to you. Let no one go without prayer, in particular, the prayer that I left in legacy to My body of believers.

Keep the vision of My Cross before you as you recite these holy words in prayer.

Our Lady

My children, go out and bring the unsaved to my Son. Let them know of my love for them. So many remain in this world of lost souls. It seems that no one can separate these stray sheep from their materialistic way of life. Soon events will come upon them and shake them from this passing world. Then, and only then, may the light of my Son be able to reach them. Some will succumb, but the majority will be lost forever. Let all that I have taught you, these many months, become alive as you attempt to lead these stray little ones to my Son.

I will remain your prayer partner as long as you pray. Persevere in the knowledge that my Son hears all prayer and will answer, according to His Divine Will.

(561) 6/12/93

I can feed to you, My gifts and My graces, only as you are able to digest them, according to your faith.

(562) 6/13/93

The enlightenment you ask for will come upon you at the moment it is needed. You will be aware of what to pray for, as My Spirit will prompt you thus. Live each day for Me, My son, then you will always be prepared for ministry. Spread My Good News wherever the opportunity presents itself.

(563) 6/17/93

Have I not brought about all of which I have spoken? Continue to pray and obey and all will come forth, according to My Will.

(565) 6/19/93

...Listen to the words that I will have for you prior to the night of prayer. There will be words of wisdom to assist you as for what you are to pray. Listen intently, so that you will hear My voice as I speak to your spirit. Be still and know that I reign supreme in your heart and that all I reveal to you is what has been told to Me by My Father.

My Mother comes to strengthen and support you as you go to battle against the forces of this world and against the evil one. Persevere and know that We are with you.

(570) 6/26/93

Yes, I am your Lord, your God, your all. Without Me you can do nothing, with Me, you can do all. Believe in the works of which I have commissioned you to fulfill and you will see wonders not seen before.

Come to the water, My son, and drink!

(571) 6/28/93

The gift is yours. You will feel the knowledge. You will know of what infirmities to pray for, whether spiritual, physical or emotional. It will manifest itself as you begin to pray. Be not concerned, but know that any physical feelings, on your part, come from Me. You will know!

(572) 6/28/93

Our Lady

You will be at peace this night my little son.
Together, our prayers will heal the sick, liberate the
prisoners and bring to my Son those of whom do not
know Him. Stay in an attitude of prayer and let the
Holy Spirit guide. There will be abundant fruit, this
night.

(573) 6/28/93

Our Lady

You will be led to more ministry, very soon. You are
to conduct yourself, always, in a manner befitting
the ways of my Son.

I will assist in new situations in which you are to
pray. You have seen healings, conversions, and the
increase in faith. Continue on without faltering.

(575) 7/1/93

I will give to you Wisdom as you press forward in
the battle for souls. My gifts will be given to you so
that they may be used to combat the wiles of the evil
one. Be courageous and do battle in My Name. Fight
vigorously with prayer to win souls to Me in order to
save them from eternal damnation.

(576) 7/3/93

What you will hear today is the theme of salvation.
Again, I say, go out into the harvest and bring the
lost souls to Me. Time is no longer a luxury, as we
approach the final days of these times. Heed what I
say!

(577) 7/8/93

Leave all behind which is not of Me. Come into the inner area of your soul. You will find Me there. Be ready and willing to pray wherever I send you. More churches will be open to you as I prepare hearts to accept this ministry. Stay united closely to those sent to you for the expansion of this work. Be constantly seeking opportunity to minister to My little ones, for this has always been the purpose of My mission for you — the garnering of souls for the Kingdom.

(578) 7/8/93

Our Lady

My son, whenever you call upon me to join you in prayer, I will be with you. Let our prayers bring solace and healing to those who seek the Will of my Son. Be sensitive to my presence as you call upon me. Be sensitive to the Holy Spirit, as you invoke His Presence. More marvels will transpire, as you persevere to do the Will of my Son.

Peace to you!

(579) 7/10/93

I will come and touch your heart, as you have invoked My Holy Spirit.

I touch your head with Knowledge and Wisdom which will sustain you in moments of ministry of which I have commissioned you to perform, in My Name. Always listen for direction from Me and My Mother, so that you will not stray from the fold. Peace!

(581-582) 7/14/93

Pray and do what Christianity calls for and let My

plan of salvation be fulfilled. I have called you out of the darkness to be a vessel of compassion and healing. Through My Holy Spirit will My people be brought to conversion by your yielding to My power. Your "yes" to Me is all that is needed. I will work miracles through your yielded spirit. My love and your love, combined, will win wounded spirits into the fold. Allow whatever gifts that are given to you to be used in the power of the Father, and of the Son and of the Holy Spirit. And let My love dwell intimately within you!

(583) 7/15/93

My work will be done regardless of whatever obstacles come onto your path. These are My works and no one will deter what I have planned; therefore, continue as I have directed, for all will fall into place, according to My Divine Will.

(586) 7/24/93

Be humble in all you do, as it is a sign of Me. As I was humble, so must you be humble. Humility is when you give of yourself without thought of how you may appear to others. My Holy Spirit can dwell more readily in those who practice this virtue. Be attentive to all signs that I may impart to you with regard to ministry.

(591) 7/31/93

My little son, begin tomorrow with anticipation and fervor that I will use you in such a way that there will be no mistaking that My Hand is in the center of all that transpires. Pray! Fast! Sleep in peace.

(620) 9/11/93

Be the balm to My people for which you have been
tutored. Let nothing dissuade you from this work.
You have been created for this, as has been foretold.
Listen, if you have ears.

(623) 9/15/93

My Holy Spirit will anoint you as you will become
more and more an instrument of My bidding. Keep
your eyes upon Me and My Holy Mother and all will
transpire according to My plan of salvation.

(626) 9/18/93

Our Lady

Consecrate yourself to me in a most special way and
I will be with you while you pray for healing. I will
intercede for you before my Divine Son for those of
whom you pray. They will be bathed in the light of
the Holy Spirit and will find that for which they
seek. The power from on High will be present as you
lay your hands.

(628-629) 9/24/93

Tonight, My Son, you will experience new revelation.
It will come as you minister to My people. Be alert,
cover yourself, and all, with My precious blood, as
you come against the enemy. He will try to block My
healing power, but it will be to no avail. The power
of My Spirit cannot be overcome or even matched by
earthly or spiritual beings. I Am, Who Am and there
are none above Me. I Am the East and the West, the
North and the South, I am all. I am all to all. Strive
to become accustomed to My presence, My inner
voice. Let Me lead you into the world of My silence.
I will obtain for you that which no one can give you,

pure love and pure peace. My little one, your works for Me will not be in vain for I will bring healing and conversion to My people, through you. Be diligent, persevere, pray, fast, and know that you will do mighty works in My Name. I bless you in the name of the Father and of the Son and of the Holy Spirit.

(633) 10/2/93

Call upon My Holy Spirit for enlightenment of the direction in your life, especially in the Holy Scriptures. You will find Me there to guide you in your endeavors for My glory. Let My Spirit fall upon you at every occasion that you minister to My people for the purpose of conversion and salvation. Be peace to all.

(636) 10/5/93

My people come tonight and adore Me in My Holy Presence, on this altar, in this place of worship. And for this, My heart is full of joy.

I ask all of you here in attendance to seek out others, those who are lost, and those whose hearts have become lukewarm, and show them, by your example, that it is I, your God, who comes before you in My Flesh and My Blood. Your love for Me brings you closer to your final goal, eternal salvation. I love each and every one of you and I give you the gift of My Mother.

(637) 10/7/93

My desire is to bestow happiness on My people, in whatever way I deem it to be beneficial for their well being. Continue to seek Me and continue to walk in My path, in obedience, and I will lead you to holiness.

(638-639) 10/10/93

Marmora, Canada

Share all you have with your brothers and sisters, your prayers, your love and tell them of My love for them. Those who have gathered here today, in true pilgrimage, will be blessed for their efforts to come to this place to visit My Mother. My peace and My blessings will be bestowed upon them. Even the curious and the skeptical, will receive graces, according to My Divine Will. This place is "Holy Ground" and you and the others will have a part in enhancing and encouraging the conversions that will emerge from this haven of worship. Wherever My Mother is present, the graces will flow, as the water on the hill. Be strong in your endeavors in ministry and I will bless all that transpires as you attempt to bring more souls to salvation.

Our Lady

These people who attend here today, I bless, as they are all my children. Love each of them, as I love you. In the Name of the Father and of the Son and of the Holy Spirit.

(643) 10/16/93

Fr. Swizdor will give you advice needed to assist you in the ministry which you are called. Persevere to see him and ask of him all that you desire to know in order to carry on the works in which you have been commissioned. New areas will be surfacing soon. Be prepared to meet the enemy as you continue to minister to My people. You must be armed for battle.

(644-645) 10/18/93

Come and take refuge in My Sacred Heart. There

you will find peace and, also, the answers to many things. In a short time, more changes will take place, both in the world and in the ministry. Be patient, endure whatever comes and you will be rewarded by the events to come. Your concentration should be on Me, My Holy Mother, and prayer. Listen, as We direct in all matters. Relate to the others in ministry that Our love goes out to them for their faithfulness to Our cause, the cause of conversion and salvation. The "little church" has been blessed by My Mother, and by Me. The prayers of these faithful have reached the heavens, bringing smiles to My Mother and I. Peace to you, My son.

(646) 10/19/93

Yes, view Me in awe as I speak to your heart. This day has been tiresome for you, My son, but you came anyway. This is the meaning of perseverance. Come to Me and I will give you rest.

(647) 10/20/93

Our Lady

Be always prepared to pray for the brethren, when-ever the occasion arises. This is what you were commissioned to do. All else that can be done to further conversion and salvation will be as was planned by my Son.

(648) 10/21/93

My thoughts are your thoughts and when I speak, your heart becomes My heart. Learn to listen closely to My words. You will sense deep within you when I am pres-ent and for when I wish to press you into service. Be glad that I called you by name and that I ask you to serve Me. I am pleased that you gave Me your "yes".

(654) 11/6/93

Be attuned to what I have to say, this day. Opportunities to minister will come upon you. Go wherever prayer is needed and let My Holy Spirit minister to My people. The sick will be healed, the sinful will be converted and the gifts of My Spirit will flow freely. Go, as My apostle!

(658) 11/21/93

Be uplifted and know that I will lead the ministry to victory.

You My son, must lead others to Me, meaning thus, to conversion and also into ministry, for I will bless and enhance these works beyond your expectations. The gift has been yours all along, but you must activate it. I bless all of you, in the name of the Father and of the Son and of the Holy Spirit. Peace!

(659) 11/22/93

My words will come upon you, as you pray. I have anointed you, My son, therefore be at ease and know that I will use you to minister to My people. You have come from a long line of those whom are used to further My Holy Word. I will not let you falter, as you represent Me.

Come, drink of the spring of eternal life. Be counted among My friends. You cannot conceive of what is forthcoming, as you remain obedient to My direction. I will speak to your heart.

(661) 11/30/93

I wish for you to continue to ask for My direction for without it there would be nothing. I lead you and teach you for I have need of you because of the works that must be done for unsaved souls.

Remember, always, that I am the Potter and that you are only a vessel, made of clay. I mold you into whatever need I have for you.

(662) 12/4/93

My son, keep always My commandments, so that I may work in you and through you. You have come to know Me, somewhat, and understand My love for My people and because of that love, what it is I want done to bring them closer to Me. More direction will be given to you, as you continue to listen to My voice within you. This set-back is temporary and is the work of the evil one, but you will prevail for I have need of you. You will go through more testing. It is My Will that the outcome will be in favor of My cause. Lean upon My Holy Mother for your needs. She will be your comforter.

(663) 12/4/93

(Our Lady)

My little son, you will be called upon to do more and more, for he who is given much, much is expected of him. But the Spirit of my Son, Jesus, rests upon you; therefore, have no fear of what others think or say, as it matters not. Only that you do the Will of God in the area of your commission. We love and protect you, always.

(665) 12/7/93

You will see the opening in the sky. The ray of light which you have not seen for along time. Be thankful that this grace will be bestowed upon you.

(666) 12/8/93

Our Lady

On this, my day, let all that I have said to all of you be heeded as I come as the messenger of the Most Holy One, the Son of God, and my Son.

(668) 12/16/93

I call you, tonight, to reinforce your allegiance to Me. I want you, again, to state your loyalty as My follower. Let nothing dissuade you from the truth. Let all that I have said unto you, come to life.

Live the Gospel for My sake. Let the works that you do in My Name, be fruitful and bountiful. I bless you in the Name of the Father and of the Son and of the Holy Spirit.

(669) 12/17/93

Lest you forget that it is I who gives you life and it is I who leads you in the path of righteousness. Without Me you are nothing, with Me, you can be all. Pray fervently and be united to My Sacred Heart and the Immaculate Heart of My Mother. Peace.

(670) 12/18/93

Our Lady

My little son, you have been called to ministry, and though it seems, at this time, that doors appear to be closed, be uplifted, and know that My Son, Jesus will open the doors when the time is right. He has not brought you to this point in time, for naught. Persevere and continue to seek and you will find the works which are to be done.

(674) 12/24/93

You cannot concern yourself with the world. This is not why I created you. You are to be a worker in My vineyard and gather souls to My Sacred Heart. This is the reason for your existence. All else is of meager importance. Let My spirit of Love dwell within you so that My people may see Me, through you.

(677) 12/30/93

I have brought you the peace that you have asked for. Let all that you do be for My Honor and Glory. Be patient and allow me to continue to work in your life. I will not abandon you. Let My Spirit form you into what I want you to be. Be pleased you are among My chosen.

(678) 12/31/93

Continue ministry as I have planned. Souls will be saved. Give of yourself to assist in conversion of those who otherwise would be lost.

(679) 1/2/94

My heart touched your heart so that We may be in unison. It is My desire that peace will prevail within you so that you may help others. Attempt to shed all that is negative and concentrate on your assistance to others. My love for My people will include your service to Me. What you felt was My Holy Peace.

(681) 1/7/94

There will be many souls coming to Me as you offer your prayers in memory of My Death and Resurrection. I will come to you in new forms, as you follow the path of holiness. This will be a year of happenings for those who have listened and for those who have not listened. Go in the love of My Mother and I.

(682) 1/11/94

Our Lady

I desire a further closeness with you that you have often requested. It is I who intercedes, always, for you, before my Divine Son. Your prayers and your perseverance please me and, although you stumble along the way, I will be there to assist you and cover you with my mantle to protect and defend you, as you compose a segment of my army.

(684) 1/15/94

Trust!! Again I say, trust, for only through Me can all things be fulfilled. Come to Me, always, in all of your needs. I cannot be substituted for anything of this world. Hold fast to all that I have taught you as time draws near for intense service in My Holy Name.

Be at Peace!

(685) 1/20/94

As you enter My church, pray that your prayers will be a means of healing for My people and that they will turn to Me in total conversion.

(686) 1/22/94

Our Lady

You will come, again to my Son, in the garments of white. He will accept you as you are in all of your sinfulness and wretchedness. He will pick you up, when you fall, as He is the Father to His children. He will chastise you when necessary and teach you the way to love and holiness.

(687) 1/24/94

Our Lady

You will hear what is meant for you to hear this night. Be attentive and aware that the presence of my Son will be calling my people to conversion. Pray that they may submit to His Holy Will. You will be anointed and the Holy Spirit of my Son will be transmitted through you. We bless you in all that you do for the Kingdom.

(688) 1/25/94

You have had but a foretaste of My power. There will come a time that will surpass all that has already transpired in the ministry.

Be warned, be armed with prayer and fortitude and the evil one will not penetrate My might. Continue to persevere and seek the avenues open to bring the lambs to Me, for I yearn to hold them in My arms.

I love you and all My other children who are brothers and sisters to you.

(692-693) 2/4/94

Follow your thoughts and then let it be done according to My Will. The time is approaching for more happenings in the ministry. Be cautious; however, that self does not enter onto the scene. You will know when it is My Hand that brings about the opportunities to serve Me. Conduct yourself, always, in a manner of which representation of Me will be paralleled with the life of My Glory and My Holiness. Busy times are ahead. Prepare yourself in prayer and follow all that I have taught you over these many months. I have not taken you through all these pages without purpose in My Divine Plan.

(703) 2/28/94

All will be done that needs to be done, for it will be by the power of My Spirit that will perform that which is needed. You will lay your hands and pray, I will do what is necessary according to My Will. Be strong, as I use My Power through you. There will be happenings of which I have spoken. As you pray, call upon My Name and know, as always, that My Blessed Mother prays beside you. There will be an increase in what you are to do for the Kingdom. It will start soon. Be prepared in prayer and know you will come under My Precious Blood for your protection. My Peace is your peace!

(708) 3/8/94

It is by the power of My Holy Spirit that I send you out among the people to bring healing and comfort to the afflicted. Know always, that it is through My Sacred Heart that the fruits of conversion will flow.

Go in Peace!

(711) 3/14/94

You are the salt of the earth. You are not being admonished for anything, but cleansed in the fire of My love. I wish for you to continue as you are and let all that is to occur be in My good time. You will be protected as you follow My direction in your life. You cannot move forward unless it is within My plan; however, pray also, as one to one for you are doing the works of My Holy Spirit and soon there will be the multitudes approaching the altars of My temples.

(714) 3/16/94

Be patient, My son, let Me direct all that is to occur in your life.

If you step before Me, you may not come within My Will. Know that whatever I do in your life, whatever path of which I lead you, will be for your eternal benefit.

(716) 3/19/94

I bring you a blessing and news of which you have awaited.

Be all that I have called you to be and I will continue to direct you on the path of holiness. I will see to your every need, as you trust in My Holy Spirit. The trials will be minor in comparison to what will occur.

(719) 3/24/94

Tonight will be a new experience. Pray for those who wish to return to the church, those who have been away from the Sacraments. Recommend to them that they go to confession and ask God for forgiveness and He will welcome them back with open arms (reminiscent of the parable of the Prodigal Son). This is because He seeks to bring all His lost sheep back into the fold. This is because of His love for all of us.

(720) 3/26/94

The words I now give to you are those of consolation. Know that some relief is in sight. My power will descend upon you and you will be transformed into an oasis of peace. As you pray over My people, you will obtain healing. Extend yourself for ministry, under any and all circumstances. I love you, My son.

(722) 3/31/94

In the silence of this time is when I unite Myself to the hearts of My people who come to worship Me in My Blessed Presence. It is at this moment that I pour the graces upon My people who view Me in My Eucharistic Body. Let Me infill My Children with all that is of Me and let Me dispose from you all that is not of Me. My little ones, attempt to lead the others, those who do not know Me, through the pages of My gospels. There they will come to know Me in a more intimate way, realizing that I am the Way, the only way. Let this "time of holiness" bring peace to your hearts as you remain united to My Sacred Heart and to the Immaculate Heart of My Mother.

(723) 4/3/94

You who stand steadfast at the helm of ministry, seek to pray where it would seem to be most unlikely. From this point, other opportunities will emerge. Lest you forget, that through Me, all must take place, all that must be included in My Divine Plan. Be at peace in this day of My Resurrection.

(725) 4/6/94

In this time of silence you will reflect on all that you have heard of My Work. It was by the power of My Holy Spirit that My disciples healed. It is likewise in these times, that I bestow My power on those I choose to continue the works I had begun 2000 years ago. Be true to My work, My son.

(728) 4/9/94

Be in tune with Me, My son, as we go through all crosses together – you with Me, Me with you. This is the way it should be, always.

Love Me with a solid and complete love, not with a love that is transparent.

(729) 4/12/94

You please Me, My son. Do nothing different outside of following My direction. Your obedience to Me is all that is needed.

(730) 4/14/94

There will be a continuance of prosperity. You will be self-sufficient and will labor on My behalf. I have chosen you as a vessel of leadership and your course is to be the winning of souls for My Glory. Let all that you have learned fulfill that which was planned for you.

(732) 4/19/94

Look upon those who are lowly and treat them as though they were exalted, for any of them, at anytime, could be Me. Look to My little ones, the lonely, the forlorn, the destitute. As Peter said, "I give only that which I have". Do these things and the Kingdom of Heaven will be yours.

(733) 4/23/94

You have given of yourself at this time. You have endured the feeling of coldness. You did it for Me. This small act is what Father was relating to the faithful — immolation, the giving of oneself beyond the Commandments. Be at peace, My son, for more is in store for you.

(737) 5/2/94

Be just as a little one, that is the way I want you little and humble.

I will build in you an edifice that will surpass anything beyond your belief. Retain your faith and let all else come from Me. Pray and let your God govern all that will begin to transpire. All that I have spoken previously, to your heart, will come to pass. You are one of the beloved and I extend My Holy Peace to you.

(738) 5/3/94

Our Lady

Hold fast to the messages given by my chosen children. I was sent to bring the good news of mercy by my appearances throughout this world. Shortly, the grace and mercy will not be available and those who have not taken my words seriously will have to submit to the Divine Justice of my Son.

(739) 5/5/94

I will reveal to you the direction that you are to take in furthering the ministry. Do exactly as you are, with the emphasis on reaching more of My shepherds through others. You will find a way! I will be with you!

(744) 5/13/94

I will help you to obtain all goals necessary to follow My path in the seeking of souls for salvation. Seek in every place and I will find for you.

(748) 5/25/94

The direction is being shown to you, do you not see My Hand in ministry? More opportunities will become apparent and you will toil in My service, the service of love and compassion for those to which you are to minister.

(751-752) 6/5/94

It is I who lead you in this path of holiness. Nothing you can do or say, no action on your part, can substitute for My direction in your life.

Your ministry will gain power, My power, and explode into an area not expected. The ministry will flourish under the banner of My Holy Name.

Many will come to you for relief of their sicknesses, burdens, and needs. You will represent Me in a manner befitting My Kingdom. Call always on My Blessed Mother as your prayer partner and know that, with her, the keys to My storehouse of miracles will be given to you. I love you and I bless you in the Name of the Father, and of the Son and of the Holy Spirit.

(757) 6/14/94

The new day approaches with a turning point in your life. You will be blessed anew according to My Will. Be open, rejoice and know that I, Your Lord and Savior, am with you wherever you are, whatever you do, and will direct you in all your endeavors for the cause of My Kingdom. Be patient, still, and let all the events, which are to occur, come about as I intend.

(760) 6/24/94

You cannot serve Me if the world causes a wall between us. You must have complete trust. Put all in

My Hands, My son, and I will lift you to heights which you cannot even imagine. Let My Spirit permeate your entire being and know that I love you with a Father's Heart and I ask that you love Me with a son's heart.

(761) 6/25/94

Meditate on all that has come about these past few years. Know that you are where you are because of My Mercy and Grace. It is of My Holy Spirit that you are allowed to serve Me in the mission I have given you. Proceed, go forward and be assured that I will ask more of you.

(763) 7/2/94

Consecrate yourself to My Sacred Heart and to the Immaculate Heart of My Mother. Be immersed in Our love. Do what you feel you should and that will suffice. I am calling you to a higher plane and this is the reason for the continued persecution. Take heart and know that you will be within the Two Holy Hearts. I will send you peace.

(764-765) 7/4/94

You will be complete and whole. Patience is the virtue which enables you to persevere. Be grateful for this virtue for it is in persevering that your holiness will increase. I will come to you in moments of anguish and despondency; therefore, know always that I will be with you on this, your special day, and on each and every day of your earthly existence. I will replenish your strength and direct you in My ways. You will be used as My instrument of conversion and healing, according to My Will. My Holy Mother will be close to you to protect and encourage you as you serve for the cause of My Blessed Name.

You will succeed in My works, in the midst of all adversities, for My power will precede you in this ministry.

Our Lady

My Son's words have shown Our love for you. Take this love and give it to others so that, in these times, they may come into the fold before the ending of this era of Divine Mercy. I will pray with you as you pray over them and the fruits will emerge for the glory of my Son.

(768) 7/15/94

Be in control of all your actions. Let no one lead you astray. He roams as a hungry lion in search of souls to devour. Stay united to the two Holy Hearts and all protection will be yours. Let My Spirit reign within you.

(770) 7/19/94

Listen to what I say to you now:

The ADVICE is to seek Me in deeper prayer.

The DIRECTION is to continue to allow Me to lead and to open whatever doors through which you are to enter.

The ENLIGHTENMENT is that I love you and will guide you always.

(771) 7/21/94

Our Lady

You will be blessed in coming to visit my holy places where I appeared to those who would relay my words to this world. I will come to you as Our Lady of All Peoples. Look to me, always, as the mediatrix.

(772) 7/23/94

Our Lady

In your heart will be placed an image of me. This will remind you that you are to pray from the heart to my Son, Jesus. All who pray this way will have a special place with me and my Son. Let your heart guide you "where your treasure is, there is your heart".

(774) 7/25/94

St. Francis

Strip yourself of everything as I had done. Start anew into a new life, following the path of our Blessed Savior. Listen to the words in my "prayer of peace". You will be blessed as I was to become a follower of He who is ALL LOVE. We are all brothers to the one who gives us salvation.

(775) 7/26/94

Be true to yourself, My son. It is by My Holy Spirit that all will come to pass in both your spiritual life and in your earthly life. I said that I would give you abundant life, but this too, has its limitations.

(776) 7/28/94

I have chosen you to go forward and refresh My people. You have already seen the fruits; therefore, have no doubts that it is I, Jesus, working through you. Keep in sight, always, My son that you are an instrument, and only an instrument, of My healing power. I will continue to use you as you continue to yield yourself to Me. Go in the love and peace of My Mother and I.

(777) 7/30/94

Our Lady

He is influenced by others, but believes in the authenticity of the ministry and the gift given to you by my Son, Jesus. Continue to pray, continue to go forward as you are and let the Kingdom of Heaven guide you and solve all the problems which you will encounter as you serve my Son. Peace be with you.

(781-782) 8/8/94

As you come before Me in adoration, I will bless you, and the others, for you have come to spend the hour that I asked of My Holy Men of Old. You, My new disciples have come to keep company with Me. You are "My special ones," for you believe in the reality of My presence on this altar. Come often, and I will spread My graces among you. The times grow shorter and it is necessary that you come before Me and pray for those who need to change their lives, especially the many of My priest sons. Pray for them as their responsibilities are great as they must answer for the direction in which they lead My faithful.

My little son, have no concern of ministry, as the burden is mine, not yours. I will lead My people to you and not you, to them. Lend yourself to being in the state of grace for receiving them and I will do the rest. You are a willing vessel and that is all that is needed. I will bring those I choose into the Kingdom through you.

(786) 8/16/94

Our Lady

Marmora is true. It is those who are not instructed properly who cause confusion. Wherever I proclaim the words of My Son, there the father of lies will be.

(787) 8/18/94

When you lay your hands upon them, call often on
My Name, for it is by the power of the Name that
healing is transmitted to My faithful. This is My
commission to you; therefore, you will be used as My
instrument, through the power of My Holy Spirit.
You will be given the sense of whatever I want done
on that night. Do not be concerned, My Mother
prays with you.

(790) 8/23/94

You exude with thanksgiving for the previous night
of service to Me, yet, I have told you time and again
that this ministry will survive all obstacles which
may attempt to hinder it.

(792) 8/26/94

In your thoughts you receive words of teaching, consolation, direction and edification, which are reflected in your heart. It is our way of speaking to you.
This has been our intimate communication over
these three years and more. You have, in obedience,
tried to adhere to these words and because of this,
you have been chosen to serve, as My hands and My
voice, in the ministry of love and compassion for the
suffering souls. You will be given further responsibility as you strive for holiness, "Be holy as I am Holy".
I will never be away from you, and My Mother is
with you, as you do the works of the Kingdom.
Remain in our peace.

(800) 9/7/94

Let all that I have taught you, thus far, resound in
your spirit, so that you will persevere in the search
for souls on the brink of eternal darkness and lead

these to Me. I will render unto you and the faithful remnant, the graces needed in the fulfillment of My works. Know that My power precedes you for opening the hearts that will allow My desires to become reality. The gates of hell shall not prevail against you as I AM GOD.

(804) 9/15/94

You must be freed to do My works without impediment. My child, be aware that there are those who are in envy of you, those who call themselves Christians, those who are sisters and brothers to you. Let whatever is said to or about you be of no consequence, for it is only I, your Savior, to which you must give account. My power will overcome and surpass any obstacle which would impede your path. You are in My stead. You are representing Me. All in My Divine plan will come to pass.

(812) 9/27/94

Be not concerned for I will prevail and that is all that is needed.

Proceed as you believe necessary, pray and I will direct all.

You are My son and I want you free to do My works. I will not abandon you. It is by My Hand that you are now at this point.

Believe and trust and pray.

(814) 10/1/94

I will arrange your schedule. It will entail the direction in which you are to go in order to fulfill certain works for Me. Question not, just obey and allow Me to guide your way. It is for My Honor and Glory that you will be given additional tasks. I love you, My son.

(817) 10/6/94

Concentrate on the ways of My Holy Spirit and I will take care of the concerns of your worldly life. I said that you would be free to serve Me and that is precisely what will be. I love you, My son; therefore, your concerns are My concerns. Be at peace.

(818) 10/8/94

Follow your heart, My son, for it is there that I am. If peace returns, then it is the way it is to be. Only through My Spirit can peace reign.

Pray and ask for continued guidance and all things will be made new through My Spirit. Be calm and let My peace engulf you.

MARIAN EVENING OF PRAYER

On March 20, 2002 St. Pius X Roman Catholic Church was host to a Marian evening of prayer dedicated to Our Lady of Medjugorje. Ivan Dragicevic, one of six visionaries who has reportedly received apparitions from the Blessed Virgin Mary since 1981, gave a presentation of Mary's messages for the world. During the recitation of the Rosary, prior to Holy Mass, Our Lady appeared to Ivan, as She has on a daily basis. Ivan, now at the age of 37, is a father and husband, but still travels throughout the globe speaking and spreading Our Lady's messages of peace.

That night, we also heard from Art Boyle, a Christian brother from Boston, Massachusetts, who gave a stirring account of his cancer healing which he attributes to a pilgrimage to Medjugorje. His testimony was a powerful witness to the healing power of Jesus Christ.

Rev. Msgr. George Yiengst, who had also made pilgrimage to Medjugorje, was the main celebrant at mass. Rev. Chris Coric, Pastor of Our Lady of Bistrica Church was interpreter for Ivan. Following the mass were prayers of healing for spirit, mind and body, and for the gifts of the Holy Spirit according to the Divine Will of God.

Some time later, we received the ensuing communication from a mother regarding that Marian evening of prayer:

I prayed to the Queen of Peace that I would be able to bring my two children to St. Pius X Church and be present for Ivan's apparition of the Blessed Mother. I was really looking forward to it. I felt like the Blessed Mother was leading me there and all I had to do was say yes to her call and try to be good. I had the day off from work. I usually work the 3pm-11pm shift. I had been ill with a sinus infection and a very bad eye infection. My children had been very sick with the flu and asthma. That Wednesday morning, before my son went to school, he complained of having chest pain. I couldn't listen to his heart rate very well because my ears were plugged up with fluid. His pulse was fast. I asked him to go to the school nurse and get checked. She stated that he had a rapid heartbeat and wheezing in his lungs. I called his asthma specialist. The doctor told me to discontinue the new asthma inhaler that he was taking and have the pediatrician examine him right away. My children did not want to go with me to see Ivan. They kept making all kinds of excuses. I took my son to the doctor and we had a long wait in the pediatrician's office. There were a lot of sick kids there. The doctor stated that my son was fine now. It was an asthma attack and growing pains.

To get to St. Pius X Church from my home takes about 45 minutes driving. I don't like driving on the thruway with my poor vision and all the construction work. I nearly stayed home. When we arrived at St. Pius X it was about 6:10 p.m. The parking lot was full. A priest directing traffic told me to go to the other side of the church to see if there was some space over there. I felt like crying. I didn't feel worthy to be there, the terrible sinner that I am. I really wanted to get there early so that I could sit in the front as close to Ivan as possible. I was ready to head back home. I prayed out loud to the Queen of Peace, "if you want us here help me to find a place to park". Every parking space was taken. I was on my way out of the parking lot, when two priests very kindly waved to me to park over on the grass. When we arrived in the church, it was very crowded. There were all kinds of people there: young, old, rich, poor, middle aged and babies. I have been to St. Pius X Church a few times for the Queen of Peace Healing Masses. The Queen of Peace Ministry has a healing mass once a month. We had to stand in the back of the church because there were no seats left. I was standing right next to the confessional, so I went to confession. I try to go to confession every opportunity that I have. I want to live in the state of grace and be free from mortal sin. My children were very restless. I was present for Ivan's apparition. I imagined seeing the Blessed Mother wearing a beautiful gray blue mantle with a pink dress, white mantle. Her long shiny black hair, blue eyes, rosy cheeks smiling and praying, speaking to Ivan. I thought of the Queen of Peace standing there before Ivan with her arms held out to him and the people there giving everyone her heavenly blessing. During mass I received communion. I prayed for the healing of my children and self. Fr. Chris Coric from Our Lady of Bistrica Church was there to interpret for Ivan. Fr. Chris is Croatian and is from a place near Medjugorje. I felt like Ivan was looking right at me a few times when he was speaking. He said that America is spiritually sick and we must turn back to God. Go to daily mass, frequent confession and pray the rosary everyday. My children were fussing and wanted to leave. I couldn't stay to hear all of Ivan's talk. As soon as we walked out the church my son said, "I'm sorry for the way I acted mom. If you want to stay we can go back in the church. I know how much seeing Ivan means to you." My daughter apologized too. My children were very good and very happy on the way home. **I received a healing. The chest pain subsided. My children became well.** Everyday the words that Ivan spoke go through my head. "You must return to God." I am trying. I'm trying to fast and pray more. I'm trying hard to stop sinning. I will keep working hard on my conversion. May the Queen of Peace send you all her heavenly blessing! God's peace to all.

Kate Liegl

MARIAN EVENING OF PRAYER

Wednesday, March 20, 2002

St. Pius X Roman Catholic Church
1700 North French Road
Getzville, NY

Ivan is one of the six visionaries from the tiny village of Medjugorje, Bosnia-Herzegovina. Since June 25, 1981, he has received daily apparitions from the Blessed Virgin Mary. Now at the age of 36, Ivan is a father and husband, spreading Our Lady's messages of Peace.

Beginning at 6:00 PM

Rosary and Confessions
Mass- Main Celebrant: **Msgr. George B Yiengst**
Testimony of Medjugorje healing: **Arthur Boyle**
Visionary: **Ivan Dragicevic**
Prayers for Healing: **Tony Cubello**

Prayers will be for healing of spirit, mind and body, and for the gifts of the Holy Spirit according to the Divine Will of God.

A Prayer for Healing

Lord Jesus, I give You my hands to touch those with Your love and peace.

I ask You to heal those in pain, to encourage the hopeless, to console the sorrowing, to provide for those in want.

I ask you to reach out to the lonely.

I especially plead for the many people suffering spiritually, physically and emotionally.

I give You my voice to pray over those who are hurting this night.

Jesus, You know of all the needs of Your people; therefore, we trust in Your love and Your mercy and that You will heal them according to Your Divine Will.

MICHAEL

"Then war broke out in heaven. Michael and his angels fought against the dragon, who fought back with his angels; but the dragon was defeated, and he and his angels were not allowed to stay in heaven any longer. The huge dragon was thrown out — that ancient serpent, named the Devil or Satan, that deceived the whole world. He was thrown down to earth, and all the angels with him." (Revelations 12:7-9)

Time and time again, in centuries past, St. Michael came to the rescue when dreadful wars and persecutions threatened to destroy Christianity. St. Michael has ever proved himself a valiant warrior for the honor of God in heaven and on earth. By his power he wages continuing war with Satan, in the great kingdom of God upon earth, the Church.

At every healing service, before I lay on hands, I ask that all in attendance join me in the prayer to St. Michael:

"St. Michael, the Archangel defend us in battle; be our protection against the wickedness and snares of the devil. May God rebuke him we humbly pray and do thou, O prince of the heavenly host, by the power of God, cast into hell, Satan and all the other evil spirits, who prowl through the world seeking the ruin of souls. Amen."

This powerful prayer of exorcism was composed by Pope Leo XIII; in a vision he had been shown the fearful battle to be waged between Satan and St. Michael, over the church of the future. Now, as never before, the Church needs the intercession of St. Michael. Please pray this prayer every day!

St. Michael the Archangel
(Painting by Josyp Terelya)

HIS DIVINE MERCY

This writing would not be complete without speaking of God's Divine Mercy. No deeper way does our Lord profess how much He loves us than by imparting to us the gift of His Mercy. Divine Mercy knows no bounds and pardons even our most serious sins; thus moving us to resolve not to repeat our transgressions. Sister Faustina Kowalska of the Sisters of Our Lady of Mercy in the city of Krakow, Poland was awarded the task of "proclaiming and introducing into life" the mystery of God's Mercy, and imploring that mercy for the world. This witness and life mission has been entrusted to the now Saint Maria Faustina.

Sister Faustina saw a vision of Our Lord Jesus Christ, clothed in a white garment. His one hand was raised in blessing, the other was touching the breast of His garment. From an opening in the breast of the garment came forth two large rays: one red and the other pale. The two rays denote blood and water; the pale ray stands for water, which makes souls righteous and the red ray stands for the blood, which is the life of souls. Sister Faustina was later instructed to paint an image according to her vision of Our Lord with the inscription "Jesus, I Trust In You". Jesus said to Faustina "I desire that this image be venerated...throughout the world".

As a further sign of His forgiving love, Jesus called for the "Feast of the Divine Mercy" to be celebrated in the whole church. He said to Sister Faustina "I want this image to be solemnly blessed (the second Sunday of Easter), that Sunday is to be the Feast of Mercy. On that day the depths of My Mercy will be open to all. Whoever will go to confession and Holy Communion on that day will receive complete forgiveness of sin and punishment. Mankind will not enjoy peace, until it turns with confidence to My Mercy." Jesus further asked Sister Faustina that this Feast of the Divine Mercy be preceded by a novena to the Divine Mercy, which would begin on Good Friday. He gave her an intention to pray for on each day of the novena.

The devotion to Jesus as the Divine Mercy is based on the writings of Sister Faustina Kowalska, the simple Polish nun who in obedience to her spiritual director wrote a 600-page diary recording the revelations she received regarding God's Mercy. Sister Faustina died on October 5, 1938 at the age of 33, the same age as Christ when he died.

On April 30, 2000, Pope John Paul II canonized Blessed Maria Faustina Kowalska.

St. Maria Faustina Kowalska

Jesus, I Trust In You

The Queen of Peace